Down the Lane

to

Sweet Home USA

Benna K. Roberts Williams

Bedside Books
2389 South, 300 East, Salt Lake City, Utah 84115
www.american-book.com

Printed in the United States of America on acid-free paper.

Down the Lane to Sweet Home USA

Designed by Jana Rade, jrade@impactstudiosonline.com

Foreword by Mr. Elwin Goolsby

Publisher's Note: This publication is designed to provide accurate and authoritative information in regard to the subject matter covered. It is sold or distributed with the understanding that the publisher and author is not engaged in rendering legal, accounting, or other professional service. If legal advice or other expert assistance is required, the services of a competent professional person in a consultation capacity should be sought.

Library of Congress Cataloging-in-Publication Data is available upon request.

ISBN 1-930586-95-7

Williams, Benna "Roberts", Down the Lane to Sweet Home USA

Special Sales

Down the Lane to Sweet Home USA

Benna "Roberts" Williams

Dedication

To
William Benjamin Roberts
Dec. 12, 1892 - Nov. 8, 1988
And
Alice Edna "Reynolds" Roberts
Aug. 2, 1895 - May 6, 1966

Even though I have these precious memories of Grandma and Grandpa, I will always love and miss them until we meet again.

Foreword

When Grant County, Arkansas was created by an act of the General Assembly in 1869, the petition that was presented stated that the region would contain over five hundred male inhabitants, potential voters and 639 square miles. Families coming from east of the Mississippi River seeking opportunities unavailable to them back home had already settled parts of this new county.

Survey maps of the 1840s show that many of these settlers had cleared land and built homes in more desirable parts of the county years before its creation. As trails were cut into the region, the population grew, followed by the appearance of schools, churches and post offices.

The little settlements that clustered around these institutions often took the name of a family, a church or a post office, and in some cases, such as "Frog Level," from an open interpretation comment on the environment.

One such settlement was Pratt's Ferry, an easy-to-ford crossing on the Saline River. As wagons slowed to cross at this place, some chose to settle here, to put down roots, and to build a "Sweet Home" perhaps like those they had left behind.

These people soon learned that, in order to escape the annual flooding of the river, they would need to back away to the high ground, which afforded access to the water, yet protection from its fury.

Prattsville, due to its location near the crossing, soon became the hub or rural pioneer settlement with narrow roads or trails radiating out to even more rural neighborhoods such as Paxton, Turin, Buie, Coopers Corner, Davis Creek, Harvest Bell, Philadelphia and Sweet Home.

These tiny places retained their identities for years, although most eventually lost their schools, post offices and crossroad stores. What they did retain were the families who gave them life and who called them home.

Today, family names originally listed in government censuses taken as early as the 1830s and 1840s still appear in telephone books of a new century. Many of the people, descendants of the first settlers, occupy the same land their pioneer ancestors once cleared.

Life was at a slow pace here in these rural places, and although progress was encouraged, it was viewed with suspicion. Electricity was first supplied to Prattsville in 1935. Other service soon followed.

Foreword

It was during this time that the lives and practices of the people here began to change. What had been done the same way for generations could now be altered to allow the adaptation of convenience to a world molded by the hands of an earlier generation.

The two worlds overlapped as this change took place. A coal-oil lamp perched on a television, a horse-drawn wagon parked behind a garage, or a rusting mowing machine pushed into the corner of an abandoned pasture signaled to passers-by that change had come.

Benna Williams has recorded these changing times in her book. Her observations of life in Grant County during this time are recorded here in a "down home" style, which will rekindle memories of a time now past. Memories of brush brooms, wooden radios, feed sack dresses and old screen doors. It is important that this is done not only as a record of our own time, but as a reminder to those generations yet unborn, that others were here before. This look back to an earlier time allows us all to walk with Benna down the lane to Sweet Home U.S.A.

Elwin L. Goolsby,

Author of "Decorating the Pulpit," the history of Jenkins Ferry State Park, located in Grant County, Arkansas, the site of a major battle during the Civil War.

Director, Grant County Museum
Grant County, Arkansas Historian

Preface

Having this book published is a dream I have had for quite some time. Many years ago I felt inspired to write my memories and feelings of growing up surrounded by a loving and caring family, which included grandparents on down. This book began as a short story, which I read at a family reunion. By the time I had finished reading it, everyone's eyes were flooded with tears. Even though both grandparents were gone, everyone knew whom the story was about from the moment that I began reading. The urgency to have my true stories published seems to get stronger and stronger. There are so many stories in our family to be passed down to other generations. Alzheimer's Disease, which I fear to the utmost, seems to be an inherited condition in both sides of my family. The stories I write are true things I have lived and learned.

Recording my memories with my four siblings is very important to me at this time in my life. Once we all had married and left our parents' home, our once close-knit family had never been the same. Although, at this point in time, none of us live more than forty miles from our childhood community, everyone has a separate life to live. Since I am the eldest and have the most memories, I feel it is my duty to record our childhood.

Another project I am presently working on is a series of illustrated children's books. These are true stories of my daughter's experiences growing up with a wide variety of animals. These stories have tickled everyone from the toddler to the old. They just have to be made available to the public before I am too senile to pass them on. So far I have finished three of these and there are many others to follow.

Also, I plan to write my presentation to parents on how to appreciate a child the short time you have them. After all, aren't we encouraged to write about what we have personally lived and learned?

Contents

Introduction

Alice Edna Reynolds Roberts was a lady with many talents and a bit of a mystery to those who lived in her community. If she lived in the present, she might be referred to as a Wonder Woman. Hard work and her ability to somehow heal some common ailments are traits for which she will forever be remembered. She felt very compassionate toward all creatures, great and small. Even though she had very little formal education, she was able to teach me many things I never could have learned from a textbook.

Some people find it amusing that someone as old as I am still uses the terms of respect I was taught. Whether it is in person or on the telephone, good morning, yes sir and no ma'am are permanent terms of speech in my vocabulary. By all means, every one of us learned the term "excuse me" at a very young age. Every one of us knew it was a natural thing for an audible burp to sneak up on you, but you dang better ask to be excused for it.

Grandpa Ben Roberts was a creature of habit, mainly because he had a schedule that he followed daily. He went to bed at a certain time every night no matter who was present. He wouldn't say a word. He would just take his brogans off and head for bed. Any company could just see themselves out.

Each morning he arose at the same time ready for his coffee. Breakfast was to be on the table the same time each morning. You could set your watch by watching Grandpa. You knew it was 11 o'clock when he looked at his pocket watch and headed for the dinner table.

We had to have a sense of humor when Grandpa was around, or we would be mad at him all the time. Kidding his grandchildren was almost an occupation to him. It didn't matter if I had been on a starvation diet; he would always tell me I sure was getting fat. I never heard him call us by our correct names. He had a pronunciation all his own.

When Grandpa died just one month short of 96 years old, it occurred to me how many changes he had seen in his lifetime. Just the changes in transportation must have been mind-boggling to him. He lived from walking and horse-and-buggy days to staring at a black box in his living room while watching a man walk on the moon. I don't know if he ever really believed that the astronauts went to the moon or not.

I don't really recall seeing Grandpa drive an automobile, but there are pictures in our albums of him in a jeep. There was never really a need for him to drive because he had sons who could drive him around. He lived to see electricity invented and the telephone installed in each and every house. He must have appreciated Benjamin Franklin, because he named one of his sons after him.

Children of today will never experience the making of folklore as I witnessed it in the home of my grandparents Benjamin and Alice Roberts. They were fondly known as Aunt Alice and Uncle Ben to everyone else in the communities of Sweet Home, Dirty Ankle, Tight Wad and Jericho Road, Arkansas.

If you did not live through the Depression years, throughout this book you'll learn how it affected the lives of the simple farm families and how they survived.

The secret recipes these Arkansans used for their daily necessities, such as lye soap, lard, and preserving techniques for their meats and vegetables can be found recorded here in these pages. These memories are recorded straight from the mouth of someone who lived and learned from her elders.

Our parents' motto, I guess, was the family who plays together, stays together. We may never have seen Mickey Mouse or Old Faithful, but we have unlimited memories of deer camp, fishing camp and other economical ways our parents used to amuse us.

If you have never deer hunted the way it was done in rural Arkansas when everything was still fun and affordable, you'll enjoy my childhood hunting memories. Now you must pay lease dues and aren't allowed to stray from your leased land onto someone's lease or there will be big trouble. All of the roads we traveled and knew by name are now behind locked gates. Only members have a key to the gates.

In December of 2001, I will have lived half a century, all of those years in this area of Arkansas. When I realized this fact, my decision to share my memories became more intense. Most of these memories are ones I lived myself or are ones that have been instilled in me through the years. At the end of my first half of a century, it is very gratifying to be able to say that I have accomplished something that is this important to my family. I hope everyone in our Sweet Home family sees it as the tribute it was meant to be.

In the pages of this short book, I hope to stir memories of others, who will share their history and folklore memories of their childhood with the youth of today before all are lost forever.

Chapter One

The House
And Those Who Made It A Home

On the corner, across the road from a little country store, there was a small white house with a shiny tin roof.

It had two front doors, which allowed the cool summer breezes to flow through the screens and all through the house.

There was no sound like the slap of the screen doors, which were spring loaded, as we ran in and out. One of the elders would always say, "You're letting the flies in." Grandma was prepared for this, because she had just made a new fly swatter from a piece of old window screen. She had cut the screen and had stitched it onto the old swatter handle using large stitches of twine.

Across the front there was a porch big enough so that any number of neighborhood kids could gather there to play.

There was a hicker nut tree (hickory nut) in the front yard with a conveniently placed huge, round, grist millstone for cracking nuts nearby. It took several kids a long time to crack and pick out enough nuts for a pie or cake. All of the trouble was soon forgotten after Grandma turned that hot moist cake out of the pan.

There was also a huge elm tree that provided a fine shade to sit under in the heat of the day. Having those trees was like a gift from heaven when you were out there shelling peas or shucking corn. Sure, there were tons of leaves that fell in autumn, but they weren't allowed to gather for long before they were swept away with a brush broom. The brooms were made from brushy branches of trees, tied together with sea grass strings saved from bales of hay. They worked well on leaves, but were rough on the hands. Some people actually scraped their yards free of grass instead of mowing.

The mowers were manually powered and consisted of a round series of blades on wheels with a wooden handle. There were those who preferred to let their livestock take care of the grass problem, but you certainly had to watch where you stepped. You can understand why they preferred a yard of smooth packed dirt to a green grassy one.

Red, yellow and green metal painted lawn chairs provided an open invitation to anyone who happened to be passing by to stop under the shade of the elm tree and visit awhile. In the summer the whole family would gather here to shell peas and beans or shuck a truckload of corn. It sure seemed as though the corn got ready almost every year on the fourth of July.

Afterwards we would eat ice-cold homegrown watermelon or make homemade ice cream. The ice cream freezer had to be cranked by hand. We would cover it with a towel and one of us kids would sit on the freezer while someone turned it. If the peddler had been by and Grandma had bought some fresh peaches, we would have fresh sliced peaches on the ice cream or peach cobbler with ice cream on top. Her blackberry cobbler was good too, but it left seeds in your teeth.

When you entered the small front room, there was the fragrance of Black Cherry tobacco and Juicy Fruit gum, so you knew who was there before you saw him. He would be sitting on his worn out spot on the end of the divanette (sofa) either smoking his pipe filled with Prince Albert, Black Cherry tobacco or chewing Bull of the Woods tobacco or Juicy Fruit gum.

I can see him now puffing away and checking his pocket watch to see if it was time to watch Wrestling, Queen for a Day or the Lone Ranger while sipping from the green bottle of Mountain Valley Spring Water which he swore did wonders for your kidneys. He would be wearing a red flannel shirt with the hearing aid control in his pocket and the wire running to his ear. He used this hearing aid to his advantage.

After his TV shows were over, he could turn the aid off and never hear a noise we kids made. It seemed as though his batteries were always bad when Grandma was calling for him to do something.

He always wore khakis, high top brogan shoes, and socks that were held up by garters. This was not just an elastic band type garter but the real garters gentlemen wore to hold up their socks. Those high top brogans, garters and his one-piece summer underwear were hard items to find as he got up in years. When he needed some more Mountain Valley Water, he dug in his pocket for his little leather change purse. A replacement for that purse was hard to find also when it needed to be replaced. Behind the door was his collection of hats: for winter an orange hunting cap, for summer the straw one and for Sunday wear a fine felt.

Beside the door was the antique dresser with the huge mirror and ornate woodwork. It never seemed strange for a dresser to be in the living room. When I inherited the dresser and had it refinished, there was evidence that it had previously been many different colors. In the front corner was the television, black and white of course. In that tiny room there was always the wooden rocker by the door, an upholstered rocker with wooden arms next to the kitchen door as well as another upholstered chair.

For years there was also a big wooden radio by the kitchen door for listening to Amos and Andy, Lum and Abner or Fibber McGee and Molly. I don't believe that room was more than 10 feet by 10 feet but it never seemed overcrowded. Extra wooden straight chairs were brought in when more seating was needed. The papered walls and ceiling and the floral cork rug were not elegant but they weren't uncommon in our community, so we didn't know the difference.

Only if all the chores were done or if it was a Sunday afternoon, would you find Grandma in the front room. Weekdays she would be dressed in her print feed sack dress and always an apron. Sometimes she tied a triangle shaped scarf on her head, especially if she was working. Her cotton stockings would be rolled down to the knee and held up with an elastic garter. On Sunday she would be dressed in a new feed sack dress with a brooch of some sort pinned on it. There was always matching hat, gloves and shoes to complete the outfit.

It was an advantage to be so close to the store. When the feed truck came, we could be the first to pick what sacks of feed we wanted. This way Grandma could get enough sacks alike to make her dresses, curtains or quilts. A lot of the ladies traded sacks with each other to get enough of them alike to make something. My dad, who had worked to buy a used bicycle as a child, put this mode of transportation to good use by taking sacks around the neighborhood to trade.

We also watched for the trucks that delivered flour. Grandma used a lot of flour for making all those biscuits and teacakes. Twenty-five pounds of flour came in a pillowcase, so if you wanted a matching set of pillowcases you had to be the first to the store. On some sacks of flour you might also find a washcloth attached. Robin Hood flour at one time gave white handled knives that were dandy for peeling. I myself still use one of these.

Grandma's drinking glasses were collected from various brands of washing powder. It was so much fun when she opened a new box of oatmeal, to see which piece we could add to the set of dishes this time. Sometimes it was the deep dark green and sometimes the clear pieces. We never knew if it would be a glass, saucer or bowl. These oatmeal dishes are widely collected now as antiques. I can't resist them myself because of the memories they hold for me. At one time you could also pick out a new plate when you bought a box of tea.

The neighborhood grocer never expected payment at the time of purchase. It was just understood that he got paid when the monthly checks came in. This way of conducting business carried on after I married and until he finally retired. It wasn't uncommon for us to borrow money from him to tide us over and he would add it to our grocery bill. In his store you could purchase anything from Levi's to shoes, fabric for a new dress or hardware and plumbing supplies.

Almost everyone in Sweet Home was related either by birth or by marriage. Grandpa's sister, who lived in the house behind him, had ten children. When these children all married and had children, the community really grew by leaps and bounds. Three of her children settled and lived right down the road from her house. At one time we were kin to every one who lived on that road, so when it came time to date we pretty much had to shop somewhere besides Sweet Home.

Maybe that is where the name Sweet Home originated. When you were born and raised there, you never wanted to leave.

Pa's sister, Aunt Nancy was a small but sweet little lady. How she stood those boys of hers, I don't know. It amazes me that such a small person could even bear ten children and she cared for her and Pa's bedridden mother also until she died. As a very young child, I peeked into Granny's bedroom once. All I remember was a small lady with white hair who scared me when she spoke.

Catching Grandma sitting down was hard to do, but if you did, there was always room for you in her lap. It didn't matter that you had interrupted her quilt piecing. She would rock away and sing a song I've never heard anyone else sing. It was "Little Boy, Little Boy where'd your git your britches. Daddy cut em out and Momma sewed the stitches." Then if she was ready for you to take a nap, she would sing "Bye-O-Baby bunting; Daddy's gone a hunting, for to git a rabbit skin to wrap his little Benna in." She knew an unlimited number of hymns that were so soothing to a drowsy child. "Jesus Loves Me" sounded so convincing and true when she sang it.

She also explained the meaning of the song and how God sent Jesus out of his love for us, to die for our sins. When she was working you might hear her loudly and convincingly singing "What a Friend We Have in Jesus."

You were lucky if you were in her lap when she peeled an apple. Being a diabetic she ate a lot of fruit instead of sweets. There was an art to the way she could use a spoon to scrape the apple into a juicy pulp that melted like applesauce in your mouth. After meals she would cut us a twig from a black gum tree, split and fray the ends of it for a homemade tooth brush.

I guess it worked for her. She kept her teeth her whole life. We were also taught to look the sweet gum trees over well and harvest the sticky balls of sap as a substitute for chewing gum. Honeysuckle blooms not only smell good but also have a sweet nectar we were introduced to. If you pick a bloom and bite the end off you can suck the tiny drops of nectar like sucking on a funnel.

She, like someone else I know, much to my regret, had a problem with unwanted, wild coarse hairs that sprouted from time to time on her chin. We knew when she got out the wire pliers that one of us kids were going to be requested to do some plucking. I guess the local store didn't stock tweezers and I don't remember her being one to go into town to shop.

On Saturdays after washing her hair, she wanted me to roll it in pin curls using bobby pins. With all those bobby pins and wave clamps we stuck in her hair, she almost looked like she was from space. Primping was certainly not a habit of Grandma's. Evidently, I learned this trait from her, for I too would rather be comfortable than all gussied up. Preferring outside work to housework was passed on to me as well.

In their bedroom were two ornate iron bedsteads; the kind that are now widely sought as antiques, piled high with feather beds a child could sink into and almost get lost on a cold winter night. The feathers were saved from the chickens she killed and plucked for Sunday dinners.

The pillows were also homemade striped ticking stuffed with chicken feathers.

It wasn't uncommon for the sheets to be made from hog feed sacks. On washday, the sheets were rotated to cut down on the amount of wash to be done. The bottom sheets were always washed that day. The top sheets were rotated to the bottom. The fresh sheets were always put on as cover. Those feather beds were taken outside to sun and air several times a year. They were made tough to survive the beating she gave them when she took them outside to sun.

You couldn't move, so many of her handmade quilts were tucked in around you as she led you in a nightly prayer beginning, "Now I lay me down to sleep." Beside the bed there was always the long silver flashlight; which was necessary for the trips to the bathroom in the back of the house after all lights were out. You see, there were no switches on the walls of this house. It was too hard to find the string hanging from the ceiling to turn the lone bulb on in the dark. Before the days of the inside bathroom there was a white porcelain pot, with red around the outside edge of the lid, which we used at night. The next morning some lucky child was required to gingerly lift it by the handle and take it to the outside toilet to empty.

There was never heat in the bedrooms nor was there air-conditioning in the summer. The windows were open in the summer as well as the front door, which had a screen on it. I guess that was why the house had two doors leading onto the porch so the night breezes could blow through the bedrooms. You could hear and be kept awake by the night cries of whippoorwills, bobwhites, crickets or bullfrogs. Dust and noise from the gravel road could be a sleep hazard also. The bedroom window was very close to the road since the house was on the corner. Teenagers loved to get a spinning start when turning that corner.

Each grandparent had a trunk for personal belongings. Grandpa's held white long-handles for winter that had a split in the seat, and one-piece lightweight underwear, which were shirt and boxers attached for summer. There was usually an extra pair of garters to hold up his socks, a box of King Edward Cigars, Bull of the Woods chewing tobacco, pipe tobacco, and fresh Juicy Fruit gum.

Around Christmas there might even be some orange marshmallow candy peanuts or those good old-fashioned, soft peppermint candy sticks you can't seem to find very easily now. He had a way of recycling that Juicy Fruit, which was evident on his bedpost after he went to bed at night. He was also known to keep his stash of paintbrushes and sharpening files hidden from us in that trunk.

Grandma's trunk held things such as her matching hats and gloves, Bible and notes of important things and happenings. Birthdays, comings and goings of her children and friends were recorded on any kind of scrap paper available. Notes were even written in the margins around the edge of an old minute book she kept for her Home Demonstration Club.

There you could also find the name of her cows, when they were served by the bull, and when the calf was dropped.

When reading her Bible she often wrote notes of importance to herself, whether it was something of scriptural significance, medicinal, or family related. Come to think of it, maybe I inherited her desire to write. I wonder what Grandma would say if I told her I don't even need a pen or paper to write now.

The middle bedroom was occupied by the then much-confirmed bachelor uncle. In his bedroom you found the only matching furniture in the house. It consisted of a poster bed and matching dresser with a chest. The dresser had a big, round mirror good for primping and also seeing who could make the ugliest face. He always had a radio for us to listen to and still continues to collect them to this day. Benjamin Franklin Roberts, Uncle Frank for short, came home from the war physically different, but no one ever noticed. It never stopped him like it would have some, because he can still shoot, fish, and do any other task he wishes. Maybe not just like everyone else, but he will find his own way of getting it done.

If he were around you would never die of thirst for a coke just because you didn't have any money. I really only remember Grandma swatting me one time. I asked Uncle Frank for some money to spend at the store. Grandma over heard and quickly taught me that that was bad manners. He could always tell when a kid needed a trip to the river on a hot day. How could he ever kill a squirrel with so many kids tramping through the woods behind him?

One trip to hunt squirrels is still very vivid in my mind. The Texas cousins were visiting. There were four of them and four of us kids plus our parents tagging along after Uncle Frank in the creek bottoms. I really doubt this was a serious squirrel hunt but more of a way to get eight kids out of the house so Grandma and Grandpa could rest. Most of us had already jumped off an embankment and over the creek when one of the adults looked back. On the embankment there was a humongous Diamond Back rattlesnake, which we had all just jumped over. It was longer than most of us were tall. Thank heavens, there were enough guns in the group that the snake only had moments to live. I think our moms lost all their motherly traits and beat us all back to the truck.

Uncle Frank still manages to this day, although he is now past eighty, to live on his own and care for himself and his wife. Yes, he did finally marry late in life. He always said he would never marry until Grandma and Grandpa were gone, for he had pledged to look after them. But he decided Grandpa might outlive us all. There was always a fairly new Ford car or truck available to me in his garage.

One car in particular, which I'll never forget, he lent to me for my driving test, to apply for a job and to make the quick trip to the hospital to have my baby. It seems strange that now late in his life, he has a brand new Buick in his garage instead of a Ford. He said he always wanted to try a Buick and that this would be his last new car.

Chapter Two

Christmas in the Country

There weren't a lot of Christmas gifts that I can remember at this house, but trimming the tree to put in the front window sure was fun. First we had to search the woods over for the perfect cedar tree to decorate. Holly with its bright red berries was sought to decorate the windows and doors. Sometimes a clothes hanger would be shaped into a circle and a wreath of cedar and holly would be constructed to hang on the front door. It could be seen from inside and out because the top half of the door was glass.

We kids would tramp up and down the hills and hollers trying to keep up with Grandma till she spotted the perfect tree and holly. Usually someone shot some mistletoe down from a tree for us. The dark green mistletoe with its white berries was balled up and hung over the doorways. You could kiss anyone who stood under it.

The tree was trimmed with sweet gum balls that were plentiful and could be gathered from the ground and painted either silver or gold. Bottle caps from the store were covered with the foil from Grandpa's Juicy Fruit gum. A foil-covered star adorned the top. Although these trees never had electric lights, they would still glisten as we decorated each branch with the old-fashioned silver icicles. I seem to recall a few attempts to string popcorn for the tree; however, more popcorn was eaten than strung.

This tree never seemed out of the ordinary to me as a child, but it seems to be now for some reason. Oranges, apples and all kind of fruits and nuts were abundant during Christmas. Of course there were the usual candy canes and other hard Christmas candies we kids enjoyed. One uncle always insisted on a cake with white frosting covered in chopped up peppermint. It is different, but very good.

If we were fortunate enough to have a white Christmas, snow ice cream was a treat we all enjoyed. I still keep the ingredients on hand, but we seldom have enough snow to make this old time favorite. To make a really good batch, you have to use evaporated milk, eggs, sugar and vanilla. This is poured over a large bowl of snow. If a child was greedy and ate too fast, a splitting headache would be their reward.

Holidays were so much fun then. It meant out-of-town cousins would be around for a couple of days at least. Guess what! The more children there were around, the more mischief we could get into.

Even though our family lived close by, we expected to be able to stay at Grandma's just like they did. Grandma just crammed as many as she could in each bed and the leftover children either slept on pallets or were sent to our house at bedtime.

I'm sure the holidays weren't nearly as much fun for the adults, because the amount of food prepared was unbelievable, not to mention all of that dishwashing by hand.

Fifteen to twenty children at one time in that small house were enough to make anyone crack. The ways we could entertain ourselves were endless and I don't recall us being underfoot in the house, unless it was mealtime or we were sneaking something from under the tablecloth.

Although Grandma never showed anything but love and patience toward us, I am sure she must have heaved a sigh of relief when the last carload of her grandchildren left.

Chapter Three

Games We Country Children Played

Our toys there consisted of a string with a button on it, which we could twirl from end to end. Grandma used long string tied in a loop to teach us to make Jacob's Ladder, cup and saucer and others I can't seem to remember. The same string could be used to wrap around our wooden tops, which we spun on the front porch. I suppose, if strings were scarce, we could have used that string on our wooden yo-yos also. Whistles were carved for us from cane or other tree branches.

I never mastered the game of marbles, which the boys played down on their knees in the dirt, but I was a whiz at Ball & Jacks. My mother can probably still beat me, though we would both have to be helped up off the floor now. Jump rope was played a lot in that yard on the corner. There was an abundance of the sea grass rope from the bales of hay. We would braid these together and make a dandy jump rope. I liked to watch my brothers try to keep up with us girls in jumping hot peppers.

This was when the rope was swung as fast as you could swing it. Their bare feet got rope burned a lot. We girls would be singing something like this, "Marvin and Kathy sitting in a tree, K-I-S-S-I-N-G, first came love, then came marriage, then came Marvin pushing a baby carriage."

Another favorite tune the boys liked to jump to was, "Cinderella dressed in yellow went up stairs to see her fellow. How many kisses did he get?" This was when the hot pepper jumping began. The amount of times they could jump the rope represented kisses.

A favorite jumping tune for the girls was, "Down in the valley where the green grass grows, there sat Belva sweet as a rose. She sang, she sang, she sang so sweet, how many boyfriends did she get."

At a very young age, we girls learned to rake leaves or pine straw in rows to form a playhouse. We made mud pies and tried to convince the younger ones to take a bite. The first time we turned our backs, of course the boys tore up our playhouse and we started all over.

There aren't many children now who can use their imagination and entertain themselves. Tire swings and bag swings were great for keeping us occupied. Toe sacks (burlap feed sacks) were filled and tied to the end of a rope hung from a tree limb. It was so much fun to see how many could pile onto that sack.

The favorite swimming hole, Steep Bank Ford had a cable swing all the community kids used on hot days. We would be so hot if we happened to walk to the river or ride our bikes carrying the old patched tire inner tubes we loved to float on. You were really popular at the swimming hole if you were lucky enough to have a tractor inner tube.

One of our favorite things to do was to stand in someone's hands while they threw you high into the air only to land with a great splash. Some of us who were built sturdy enough were used for diving platforms. Others would climb on your shoulders and dive into the water. Sometimes if there were two on shoulders at the same time, they would proceed to wrestle until one was thrown off. It was a true test of balance for me to keep my person on my shoulders. I couldn't even walk into the river barefoot now. I guess our feet were tougher then from going barefoot all the time. We would cool down during the swimming excursion and be hot and dirty again by the time we got back home.

If it were Sunday, sometimes we had to clear out of the swimming hole because Sweet Home church came to baptize someone. At that time our church didn't have a baptistry. I myself was baptized in the Steep Bank Ford swimming hole of Saline River. The common mode of baptism now is in the baptistry of the church, but some converts still prefer the river. Even though our church was given permanent rights to have baptisms at Steep Bank Ford, there is now a locked gate, which would have to be opened by the gate owners. Some people have no sense of tradition. In order to swim there, I guess you could climb over the gate if your desire to swim were strong enough. That is a possibility I'll have to consider.

Those Prince Albert cans were great to flatten and nail onto the end of a stick. The boys used these to run around the yard pushing metal wheels. This never made much sense to me.

Wooden dynamite boxes made fine wagons for us to haul our icebox watermelons in, or even a litter of kittens. Usually the old hound dog Lonesome or Queen would be tagging along. Dogs and cats lived in harmony in that yard, along with the wild bunch of neighborhood kids.

There were numerous games we played outside. Hopscotch was loved by everyone as well as Red Rover, Ring around the Rosey, London Bridge, Statue and Hide & Seek or Chase. At birthday parties I remember playing a game called Drop the Hankie that was simple but fun. Red Light, Green Light, Simon Says, and Mother May I were games everyone knew how to play then. Parents weren't bothered by children who were bored and had nothing to do. We knew how to entertain ourselves. We would form two lines facing each other to play Red Rover. One side would, for example, chant, "Red Rover, Red Rover, let Eddie Lee come over." Eddie would run across to the other line and try to break through the line where we would be holding our hands tightly clasped. We would never let him break through and he had to join our side. It always made him mad because he wanted to capture one of us to take back to his side.

When an argument broke out, Grandma would step in and make us hug and kiss each other. You tried to do your fussing and feuding when she wasn't around, I tell you. There would be a lot of spitting and wiping your mouth off if you were one of those who had to kiss and make up.

My Dad had another approach when my brothers were fussing. They had to put on the boxing gloves he had bought and resolve their differences that way. It didn't matter to him that Scrooge had such long arms he could put his left glove on Pudge's head and punch away with his right. Pudge was too short-armed to even reach Scrooge.

Looking back now, I wonder how the community could stand it when we played Annie Over or why we would even want to play that game. One kid would stand on one side of the house while the rest of us were on the opposite side. We would all holler "Annie-ee" and the kid on the other side would holler "O-verrr." At that time he would throw the basketball over the peak of the house to us. We never knew where it would come rolling down the tin roof. The object was that we weren't to ever let the ball touch the ground. Now, can you imagine how noisy that was to the old people who lived in that house with a tin roof and also to the close knit community all around there?

The first one to see a fresh doodlebug home in the dust or sand took a stick and stirred it round and round the funnel shaped hole while chanting, "doodlebug, doodlebug, fly away home, your house is on fire and your children are all gone." I don't even know what that was all about. It was just something Grandma taught us kids to do.

The fun didn't even stop after dark, for then it was time to catch the lightning bugs and put them in a jar to use for a night light in your room. We never worried about snakes, even though we were barefoot and in the yard after dark. When we grew tired enough to go to sleep at night, it wasn't because we were tired from watching TV or a computer; it was because we were exhausted from all the strenuous playing that day.

You washed your feet, said your prayers and usually went to sleep before Grandma could finish telling you Little Red Riding Hood or the Three Little Pigs. If Grandma washed your feet, she would pull your toes and say "this little piggy went to market, this little piggy stayed home, this little piggy had roast beef, this little piggy had none, this little piggy went wee, wee, wee all the way home."

After she had finished the daily crossword puzzle from the paper, I could usually convince Grandma to cut some more paper dolls from the newspaper. The way she folded the paper in an accordion fashion and cut the different shapes, they always came out different. When she unfolded it, the finished product would be a string of paper dolls all holding hands. Sometimes she would cut girls with dresses on and sometimes boys with their pants on. In her eyes, men were to wear the pants and ladies dresses.

While she was folding and cutting paper dolls, I would be in her wooden rocker legs spread apart, rocking away. Usually she would have to remind me that nice little girls are to keep their dresses pulled down and legs together when sitting. This rocker is one of my prized possessions but it doesn't seem nearly as big now.

Chapter Four

Grandma's Country Kitchen

I always wondered why her pie safe, painted that old-fashioned green color, and never locked up at all, was called a safe. Nothing she ever put there was safe from us. The teacakes, molasses cookies and fried pies disappeared as quickly as she put them there, but I never heard her complain even though she couldn't eat them herself.

Grandpa ate All Bran every day to keep him regular he said, so Grandma started making him All Bran muffins. None of us were too fond of them, so they were safe in the safe.

There was always milk churning, butter molding, canning or cooking going on in that kitchen. I'm just now beginning to understand how she must have felt when that electric churn came along. I have that electric churn and would love to try it out, but can't seem to find anyone who milks a cow anymore. There was always someone dropping by to purchase her butter, buttermilk or eggs.

One summer our family moved to Louisiana. We finally had gotten a car with air conditioning. I guess we didn't have an ice chest, because Dad would ice down a bucket of Grandma's fresh homemade butter she shaped in the wooden molds and we would hang the bucket in front of the air conditioner in the car. This would keep it cool until we reached Shreveport and sold it for her.

The commonplace happenings I witnessed there as a child are lost arts now. Why didn't I notice more closely how to make the butter, hominy, biscuits, dumplings, teacakes and fried pies? We didn't realize then, that the pickles and leftover cornbread we snuck out from under the tablecloth to go with our onions we pulled from the garden were really left there on purpose specifically for us.

That fresh fried chicken was a favorite of mine. After frying it in a cast iron skillet, she would pour off the fat and add a little water to the skillet, plop a lid on it and let it soften, so Grandpa could chew it. Try this sometime; it gives the chicken a mouth-watering flavor through and through.

My favorite part of the chicken is still the pulley bone. When you cut up a chicken the way Grandma did, you cut a piece off the breast some people call the wishbone. After eating the meat, you could hold one end of the forked bone and someone else would hold the other. You both made a wish and pulled on your end of the bone until someone's broke. Whoever was left with the longest bone was supposed to have their wish come true.

I'll never be able to wring a chicken's neck and chop its head off like she did. That fried chicken, chicken and dressing and chicken and dumplings I loved, were a chore for her to prepare from start to finish, but it was an everyday way of life for her. Maybe I wouldn't have such a weight problem today if I had to work that hard for my food. Yes that church bench behind the table was my sitting place for many feasts in that kitchen. Somehow I could never bring myself to taste the squirrel after watching her skin them and then the elders cracking the heads open to get at the delicacy they said was inside. The leftovers were left on the table and covered with one of Grandma's many tablecloths just in case someone stopped by unexpectedly.

In the corner of the kitchen there was always a churn of milk sitting to clabber so she could churn it to make butter. At times there was also a crock of cucumbers in the process of becoming pickled. I loved to sneak bites of that smelly cabbage in the other churn. She would gather the cabbages from the garden and after they were chopped, she would pack a churn with cabbage and salt. This would over a period of days develop a pungent smell and a sour taste, hence the name sauerkraut. She would then can it in jars for us to feast on all winter.

Beside the stove there was a 5-gallon slop bucket used to collect the day's scraps to be fed to the hogs. For a period of time we would go to a place about twenty miles away, which sold old bread and snack cakes in huge dog food size sacks for one dollar per sack. Everyone pretended we were getting it for dog and hog food, but we kids sure got to eat a lot of cupcakes before the dogs or hogs ever saw them.

Water was heated in huge dishpans with washing powder added for dishwashing. If you try washing dishes with clothes detergent, you'll understand how slick this feels. This must have been before the days of liquid dish detergents.

A metal water bucket held drinking and cooking water. The metal community dipper would be a health hazard today.

Drawing water from the well was a chore that had to be done many times a day, before Grandma's sons installed a water pump, sink and bathroom. She probably felt she was in hog heaven that she did not have to bathe herself or us in that washtub any longer. In the summer, the washtub was put out in the sun and water was drawn from the well. The sun warmed the water for our bath. No wonder Grandpa delegated only Saturday as his day to bathe. I really tried to get my bath before my brothers. You see, everyone bathed in the same tub of water and you never knew what one of those boys would do in the water.

After I married I tried bathing in a # 3 washtub again. It was quite an experience, I can tell you. Some say the old days were the good ole days. Just let them try bathing in a washtub again and they will change their mind.

Grandma also kept a wash pan of water, some lye soap and a towel on the back porch. Everyone was required to wash up out there before meals. The men and boys also knew to remove their hats before sitting at her table.

In Uncle Frank's room was the wall of shelves where all the pickles, canned soup and vegetables were stored. I never remember running out of those big dill pickles of hers.

Homemade canned soup is still a favorite of our family. You have to time soup canning so that most of the garden vegetables are ready to be harvested at the same time. One year my Mom and I timed it just right. Everything was ready: the potatoes, tomatoes, peas, okra, corn, butter beans, peppers, carrots and onions. We kept peeling, shelling, shucking and chopping all one day until we had nothing big enough to mix the soup in. I ran to town and purchased a big plastic child's swimming pool. We washed and scalded it and put it in the middle of the kitchen floor. When Dad came in from work there was a swimming pool full of soup ready to be canned in the middle of the kitchen floor. Guess what he had for supper that night. It took many jars and hours to can that much soup, but it was well worth the trouble when you needed a quick meal on a cold day.

Chapter Five

The Southern Sleeping Porch

Across the back of the house was the sleeping porch with windows all around and three beds in a row. It was here that a kid could sew on the old treadle machine if she were coordinated enough to pump it back and forth with her feet. You might even sit on the floor and operate it with your hands while she tried to sew. There usually was a quilt in the frames, because Grandma hand pieced quilt tops all the time. A kid could quilt leaving all the knots on top and she never pulled those stitches out. You see, the proper way of quilting is to bring the needle up from the bottom and pull the knot so it is hidden between the bottom and top of the quilt in the cotton.

Some of her favorite quilt tops to piece were Trip Around the World, Heart and Gizzard, Bow Tie, Nine Patch, Fan, Flower Garden, Double Wedding Ring, and many, many others. There was even one pattern that looked like a turtle. The black and white turtle quilt I own is so threadbare I'll never use it again as cover. Its sentimental value makes it a priceless heirloom. All the quilts I have, that she pieced, are treasures to me. I see bits and pieces of fabric that remind me of some dress she had, or maybe even a piece of something she made me is stitched in it to be forever remembered. Here in this sleeping porch you were never expected to sleep alone. She would lie there with you, maybe listening to the rain on the tin roof and tell all kinds of bedtime stories until you nodded off.

It was here that she stayed up with me all night once, after I became so sick that my stomach ejected my supper. Children then were not introduced to the cold truths of death at a young age. It had been a shock to me when I visited the funeral parlor for the first time, to view the body of a friend's father. It was she who explained death and the hereafter to me as she held me sick and shaking all night. Somehow that made it a little easier for me, when, as the custom was in those days, her body was brought home for viewing after her death. I could remember the words of comfort she had soothed me with that night. It was also in this room where it is said she caught my little brother munching down on the sack of dog food.

Chapter Six

Backyard Business

Usually when she opened the back door, there would be a cat named Flossy or Flo or some other such name waiting for her, to show her what game they had caught, whether it be mouse, lizard or rabbit. They would get in trouble if it were a bird, for the lady of this house loved birds, especially mockingbirds. All the boys around knew not to use their B.B. guns in her yard. One of my girlfriends, who lived across the street, hid behind her storm cellar one day with her B.B. gun. I don't know what she was aiming for, but the B.B. came through the front room window of Grandma's house.

Out in the backyard was the washhouse with two big, black wash pots in front. These were used for boiling clothes, making hominy from corn and cooking out hog fat to make lye soap. The ashes from the fire were used in the pots when making hominy. This process loosened the hull from the kernels of the dried corn.

Inside the washhouse were the wringer washer with two rinsing tubs, one with bluing and the other without. I recall the bluing bottle had a cork stopper and the picture of a lady on the label. I wondered if such a thing still existed and actually it does. The name of it is Mrs. Stewart’s bluing. The wringer washer was supposed to be off limits to us because of the danger of getting your fingers caught in it. More than one curious child has had their fingers rolled through the ringers.

It was here that she spent washday with kids and usually a litter of kittens underfoot. Those khaki pants didn't have to be ironed as much when she put them on those metal stretchers and hung them on the clothesline in the chicken yard to dry. The starch was mixed and everything from pillowcases to dresses, shirts, and khakis were dipped in this thick solution.

When the clothes were dry, they were sprinkled with a sprinkling bottle of water and put in the freezer if you had one. Somehow the sprinkling of water made them iron easier with the Betty Crocker iron. As a child, I made money by ironing starched overalls for an uncle of mine. The sprinkling bottles were made by putting a purchased sprinkling spout, which had a cork on the end, onto a coke bottle or any sort of bottle it would fit on. Most people today wouldn't have any idea what one of these was used for.

Those big, black wash pots had several uses. After the corn was harvested and dried, it was time to use some of it to make hominy. A fire was made under the pots of water and the corn was added. Naturally this made the corn swell and begin to tenderize. The magic in this procedure was when Grandma took a shovel of ashes and added them to the pot. The ashes had the same effect on the corn as the lye that some people used. It made the husk turn loose the kernels of corn. After this procedure the kernels were rinsed clean and canned in jars to be used all winter. She also used these big pots in making lye soap from hog lard and lye. I still have her washboard, which always had a bar of lye soap on it for scrubbing stubborn stains from clothes. I remember my own Mom scrubbing dirty diapers on a rub board also. We weren't fortunate to even have a wringer washer at that time. Mom had 4 babies close together, no washer, and a well that went dry every summer. It was a common occurrence for us to be taken to the river for a bath and she hauled barrels of water home for washing dishes and clothes.

On the coldest days of winter, the big, black wash pots had a fire built under them and were filled with water for hog butchering. A hole was dug and a barrel was buried at a slant. Into this barrel the hot boiling water from the wash pots was poured. Several families took turns helping each other with the butchering tasks. Hogs were kept through the year and fattened for butchering in the winter. Maybe you have heard the saying "slop the hogs." That is because the mash they were fed and the food scraps they loved did look like slop.

After the huge animal had been shot in the head or sometimes knocked in the head, it was picked up by several men and lowered into the hot barrel of water. After it was good and scalded, all the hair had to be scraped from the skin. Some people cleaned the entrails and saved them for chitlins (chitterlings), which can be bought by the bucket in supermarkets today. They are fried and are said to be a delicacy to behold. I don't think I was ever subjected to these as a child, but who can be sure. Nothing was wasted at butchering time. Ears, feet and tails were even put to use. Grandma would boil the head to make hogs head cheese or souse meat out of varied parts. Can you imagine boiling a head and picking the meat off it, much less being able to eat anything made from it? I also recall some eating pork brains and eggs mixed together.

The feet were cleaned and pickled. These are still sold in supermarkets as well and they are called what else, but pickled pigs feet. My job was to stir the big black pots of fat which was melted to use throughout the year when cooking. This procedure was called rendering lard. Doctors now probably wish this could be outlawed, since pure lard is at the root of high cholesterol levels.

I was stirring the pots one day and handling it pretty well until the entrails were added to the pot. My stomach just couldn't take that smell and sight. This ruined my taste for breakfast food for a long time. I could just smell bacon frying and get sick.

After the fat had all melted, the skins that were left floating were strained out and used as cracklins in cracklin cornbread. Cracklins can still be bought today and I love my mom's cracklin cornbread with beans. Certain portions and trimmings of the meat and fat were ground with a hand turned meat grinder to make sausage. Grandma would add some of her homegrown sage and cayenne pepper to season it just right. She would fry a patty of it and have someone sample it until she got it seasoned just right. If you ate too much of that fresh pork it had a tendency to make you sick.

After working around all of the gore, I didn't really want any meat until much later in the year. Before slaughtering time a strong wooden box was built from the heart of some good red oak lumber. Great care was taken to make sure it was air tight enough to keep out insects and rodents. The hog was cut into sections such as hams, shoulders, midlin and jowls. At least one inch of white meat curing salt was put in the bottom of the box. The pieces of meat were laid on this salt leaving a two-inch space around each piece so the meat would be one hundred percent covered by salt. The meat and salt were layered in the box until it was full. The contents were covered with a white cotton cloth and the box lid was sealed tight. The meat was left in the salt for twenty-one days. When it was removed, each piece was washed to get the salt off the surface. It was then hung in the smokehouse draining for one day.

Some type of fire pit such as a metal tub or cast iron wash pot was used to contain the fire, which was built of dry wood with small pieces of green hickory or the heart of red oak wood added. This was not a blazing fire but one that smoldered and created a lot of smoke. If the fire got too hot it was sprinkled with water. The meat was hung close together, but not touching, over this smoldering fire. The idea was for the smoke to get to all surfaces of the meat and be able to saturate it through and through with hickory smoke flavor. The fire was stoked and kept burning for about two weeks until the meat was golden brown. Most folks would leave the meat hanging in the smokehouse and cut off what they needed for daily use.

Some kids (and adults too) were guilty of cutting off chunks to eat when no one was looking. On warm, damp days a small fire would be built under the meat, which was said to keep it from spoiling. Sometimes for a different taste, sugar-curing salt was used on the meat using the same procedure as above except the meat was only smoked for seven days.

The sausage, beef and anything that needed to be frozen could be taken to Sheridan slaughterhouse. Everyone knew it as the locker plant, because you could rent a cold storage locker there. At that time, no one had a freezer at home.

The last home-smoked meat I remember eating was great and it was given to us by an old family friend in exchange for some work my husband did on his house. This was much more rewarding than any money would have been. Those old-timers always knew how to trade and barter to get what necessities they needed.

Chapter Seven

Mmm, Mmm, Good!

Salt meat is great fried and eaten with great northern beans and cracklin cornbread and of course fried potatoes and sauerkraut or turnip greens and maybe even fried green tomatoes if Grandma had her fill of ripe tomatoes. Sometimes we had fried and boiled okra instead of kraut. I had to develop a taste for the boiled okra, but now I love it cooked on top of purple hull peas. I guess not many children love something that's green and slimy that slides down your goozle without you chewing it.

No one knew then what all that fried food was doing to our arteries, but Grandma ended up dying of cancer and Grandpa lived just a couple of years shy of 100, so who knows if it is truly all that bad or not. Grandma did eat a lot of oatmeal but she always had homemade biscuits and sausage, bacon, gravy and eggs for the rest of us. Maybe that strong coffee Grandpa sipped from a saucer was his secret of longevity. He always poured his coffee into his saucer and sipped it.

I still have a plate and the creamer to her set of dishes. It is cream-colored with gold trim. Something very strange but wonderful has happened as I am writing this book. A neighbor friend of ours was going to throw away a box of dishes so he asked my husband if we might need them for our camper.

Well, when my husband took a look and saw they were antique, he brought them home. He never dreamed I would be so thrilled. The dishes were odds and ends of the same dishes I had of Grandma's. I have no idea where the rest of hers are or who had previously owned these pieces. What do you think the chances are of this happening while I am writing a book honoring my grandparents? I don't remember her having any other set of dishes until later when she got a new house; someone replaced it with a set of brown plastic. Grandpa still preferred his old cup and saucer.

Chapter Eight

Gee Haw, Gardening

Behind the washhouse there was always a garden with flowers growing among the vegetables "to keep the bugs out" she said. Grandma loved flowers. I was weeding for her one day and felt something in the handful of weeds I had just pulled. When I dropped them there was a big snake with its head flattened and hissing at me like a cobra. You never heard a kid scream so loud. Grandma came running with her garden hoe. By the time she got there the spreading adder had let all his air out and he was not much bigger than a night crawler fishing worm. I swore that it couldn't be the same snake.

You could pull all the onions, Tommy-toe tomatoes or ice box melons you wanted out of the garden, but "don't pick the green tomaters boys." Fall was the time of year there was always a garden full of turnips and greens. As a child I never liked the greens, but I sure loved to pull a turnip right up out of the ground, peel it and eat it raw as you would an apple. It's funny how when you are an adult you learn to like things like cooked turnips and greens.

In the summer you could taste the slices of fruit being dried on top of the well house, but you wouldn't taste that dried sage but once. The fruit and sage would be spread out to dry during the day and before the dew fell at night it was put in a pillowcase to be used later in making fried pies and chicken and dressing. I can still smell that dill that grew every year by the well house to be used for pickling.

I still don't know Gee from Haw, but I can still hear these commands he made to the plow horse. He would be walking behind the horse drawn plow, pulling the plow lines as they went down row after row in the garden. When the horse wasn't being used for plowing, I would saddle it up and three of us at a time would ride. It was fun then when he plowed up the potatoes and us barefoot kids would follow to pick up the potatoes and spread them under a tree to dry. Grandma taught us to pick up all those wiggly worms so she could use them for fish bait later.

Chapter Nine

Children in the Chicken Yard

There was also a chicken yard with Chinaberry trees good for climbing. We would pick the berries to shoot in our bean shooter at each other or at the chickens if no one was looking. The berries were strung to make necklaces also. Sometimes you might have an altercation with a cocky rooster, but it wouldn't take long for her to wring his neck, chop off his head and let him flop headless all over the yard. His next stop would be the dumpling pot.

In the chicken house there were always those little, soft, yellow "biddies" as she called them. I always seemed to get flogged by the set'n hen when I was sent into the dark chicken house to gather the eggs.

There was an outhouse with a Sears and Roebuck catalog inside for reading, etc. Even after the addition of the bathroom to the house, somehow the man of the house just hated to give up his trips out there.

There was one tree in particular, I remember out by the chicken yard. It was her skinning tree where she skinned unlimited amounts of squirrels and catfish. Again, maybe I wouldn't be so fat now if I had to go through all this to put a meal on the table.

It must be from her I inherited my love for fishing. Sometimes on Saturday she would put on a pair of men's khakis under her dress and pull on her rubber boots that came up to her knees. After persuading someone to take us to a pond down by the river or Nall's lake and even once to Cox Creek Lake, she'd grab her cane pole and dig some worms. She'd wade around in the edge of the water and perch jerk to her heart's content. It didn't bother her when she caught that snake and it curled around her cane pole.

Once she even taught me how to catch a crawfish with some string, a safety pin and some pork for bait.

Chapter Ten

Down the Lane to the Barn or Church

There was a lane in front of the house, which led to the barn. The barn was a great place to play. There were three stalls, a corn crib full of mice, a room for hay and that great hay loft for making play houses. It was down this lane she went twice a day carrying a bucket of water and cloth in one hand and a milk bucket in the other with me running after her. She walked carrying her milk bucket, crying S-o-o-o-k, S-o-o-o-k, to the cows to bring them hurrying to the barn. I remember two she named Pet and Brindle. They were in the family for a long time. I was expected to sit quietly up on the stall and not spook the cow while she washed the bag and began to milk. If a cat happened by, it might get a squirt toward its mouth. It was in this barn that I witnessed cows being dehorned. No one could ever convince me it didn't hurt them, when some of them bled so profusely.

It was also down this lane and through the woods, I followed her on Sunday to Sweet Home Missionary Baptist church. She would have on her best feed sack dress and hat, shoes and gloves to match. This is the only time you would see her without an apron tied around her waist. Grandma's family were originally Methodists. She and a friend slipped away and began going to the Baptist church. It is my understanding the families also converted to Baptists.

Grandma's friend later became a world-renowned, Missionary Baptist minister. I'll never forget sitting by her on the ladies side of the church, for then the men and ladies sat on opposite sides of the church. The men also had what was called the Amen corner. Those men who sat in that corner would voice a loud Amen, when the minister said something they wholeheartedly agreed with. We don't seem to hear very many audible Amens anymore.

In the summer the ladies all used the cardboard fans with wooden handles, which the local funeral home provided. They would fan and rock cranky babies as they sang. Grandma would join in the singing of those old hymns she loved. It was usually "In the Sweet Bye and Bye," "Amazing Grace," "We'll Work til Jesus Comes" or "Precious Memories." At that time, when I heard her sing "Shall We Gather at the River," I thought she was thinking of fishing.

It was my privilege to attend the one-hundred-year anniversary of the Sweet Home Missionary Baptist Church a few years ago. We still have the annual homecoming every third Sunday in April. It is a bit unusual for a Baptist church, but we have had the same pastor for over thirty years. It is a little different than it was when Grandma and I attended together.

The long row of wooden tables that were once outside under the huge spreading oak trees and used to hold all of that good home-cooked food are gone now. The meal is now served in an air-conditioned fellowship hall. There is still an abundance of talented musicians who sing and play from the old hymnals filled with songs written with shape notes. I can still hear everyone singing Do, Re, Mi at the singing schools we used to have each year. Bible School is still a big hit with the community children each summer.

We are blessed in this area to have so many churches, so close together. There are five Baptist churches in this small area. The city limits of the incorporated town of Prattsville, where we kids attended school, only has a population of 300. Everyone has skeletons in their closet, but I guess one our family has to live down is that one of our ancestors and his friends were three sheets to the wind one night and they rode down the aisle of one of the churches while services were being held. I've been told the hoof prints of the horses could be seen on the wooden floor for some time.

We also have some ancestors we can be proud of. A timber company has left a little grove of trees on their property between Prattsville and Sheridan. These trees mark the cemetery where one of our ancestors who was killed in the civil war is buried. A civil war veteran stone marks his grave.

There once was an African-American church not far from Sweet Home church. They even had a cemetery next to their church, something Sweet Home doesn't have. Cemetery or not, their church picked up and moved a number of miles away and I can understand why. I have been told that years ago, before cars were in use around here, the community boys would sneak through the woods to listen to the good singing and shouting that took place at that church.

One night, their meeting must have held on pretty late, because the sleeping babies were taken out and put in the horse drawn wagons so they could snooze away. Those hooligans were watching and decided how funny it would be if they switched the babies around. They did just that and everyone says wagons were going up and down the road all night as the mommas were trying to find the right baby. Who says the youth of today are mean?

When this area was first settled there must have been a lot of African-American people who lived and farmed this area. There are hills and hollows named for them all around the area where I live. An African-American lady, who was a wet nurse to the babies while their mothers worked in the fields, nursed Grandpa himself.

Chapter Eleven

Grandma's Doctoring Days

There remains a mystery of sorts about Alice Roberts still today. People would bring her their babies when they had an ailment then called thrash in their mouth. Doctors today call it thrush. It was a red, painful rash in the mouth and throat that made it hard for a baby to eat and swallow.

She would take the crying child and go down the lane toward the barn alone; no one else was allowed to go. Whatever she did to heal the child, I don't know, but people believed in her and said it worked. She always said she could teach only a man her secret, not a woman. There is one man alive today who knows her secret. Why can't I bring myself to ask him to pass it on? As far as I can remember she never healed me of thrash, but she always told me to call the warts on my knee, beans. One day I woke up with her rubbing these warts and not long afterwards, the warts were gone.

My other grandmother told me to bury the dirty dishrag under the doorstep and the warts would go away. I wonder which method worked.

Sassafras tree roots were dug and used to brew a tea for drinking. When we had a cold, she smeared a flannel rag with Vicks salve and warmed it on the heater to plaster to our chest when we went to bed. That would really open your head up and loosen your chest congestion. Grandpa would rather dip his finger in the Vicks and swallow some to rid himself of a cold. He swore that the smelly Ben-Gay was a remedy for his aches and pains and used it liberally before he went to bed.

When a baby was constipated, Mom would hand it over to Grandma, who would perform a soap or tea enema. That was one sight I witnessed once and never care to again. Grandma was very capable of performing midwife duties. She delivered one of her own children by herself.

A child complaining of an earache would give Grandma a reason to bring out the sweet oil. She would barely warm it in a spoon and pour it into the hurting ear. Warm cornmeal was tied up in a sock and put on the ear when you went to bed. That much attention from Grandma would make anything feel better.

Her compassion and healing were shown toward every living thing. I have heard of how she used a needle and thread to sew up a dog wounded by a wild hog. Uncle Calvin had a dog well known for his hog hunting abilities.

One of the neighbors, Mr. Tucker was having a problem with a huge wild hog rooting up his garden at night. Lending him the use of the dog was the neighborly thing to do.

One morning after the hog had been in the garden, Mr. Tucker and the dog set out to track him down. That dog immediately sniffed out the trail and ran ahead to jump on the hog. He should have waited for back up because that hog had long, sharp tusks that ripped an either brave or mighty stupid dog wide open.

Mr. Tucker gave up the hunt and carried the dog for at least a mile back to Grandma. Most people would have just put him out of his misery, but not Mr. Tucker. He hated the fact that he had borrowed the family hunting dog and now he had to face the Roberts boys. When he walked into the yard, of course everyone came running. Mr. Tucker didn't even have to tell them what happened to the dog for his intestines were spilling out of the jagged cut. He just said he didn't think there was anything that could be done for him, he just had to bring him home instead of leaving him out in the woods.

Grandma took one look and even though the dog's intestines were protruding through the jagged cut, she told my dad to fetch some water and clean rags. This tender hearted but tough lady washed the leaves, dirt and trash from that half-dead dog's wounds, taking special care to clean the intestines. With a curved darning needle and good strong thread she stitched and gradually worked the old dog's intestines back where they belonged. No fine surgeon could have done a better job.

Anyone who witnessed that probably thought Grandma could do anything. What is even more miraculous is that she nursed the dog back to health and he actually survived.

Even though I inherited some of her physical traits and will never forget some things she taught me, could I do that?

Her sense of humor still makes me smile when I remember her telling me how one of her sons, Frank, was sent with one shell to hunt for meat for supper. Evidently times were hard then. He was so thrilled when he returned with what he thought was a prize turkey. Grandma cleaned and cooked a lot of things, but she absolutely refused to cook that buzzard.

She also delighted in offering an unsuspecting kid a green persimmon. It only took one puckering bite for me to learn that she loved a good joke. After that, when we went to pick wild muscadine grapes to make jelly, it took some coaxing before I would taste them or huckleberries. The blackberries we picked were delicious in her cobblers and jelly but I don't know if they were worth all those chigger bites and briar scratches.

After I was grown and married, my husband and I picked some huckleberries from a vine in the woods. I made the most beautiful two-crust pie from scratch. It was the best looking pie I had ever cooked so I took it to share with some close friends. After one bite of that pie they suspected very strongly that I had come to poison them. I can't even begin to describe the taste. It was horrible, so horrible our dog tried to eat some and then ended up trying to scrape it off her tongue.

After an investigation, we learned that those berries were winter huckleberries and they are not edible. True huckleberries grow on low bushes. They are great when they are green in a pie and when they are ripe they make delicious jelly.

Chapter Twelve

To the Woods We Go

Sometimes Sunday afternoons were spent riding in Uncle Frank's car through the woods to Jacob's Cemetery. Our family still cares for this cemetery. With each family grave that is added, it becomes dearer to me. It is located in the heart of the woods with no houses in sight, and the peace I feel there is a comfort to me.

While Grandma picked Poke Sallet by the roadside, Uncle Frank would drive us kids up and down the road, hanging out the window looking for deer tracks. When he spotted some tracks, we would jump out to stomp the deer tracks so others wouldn't know where the best deer crossings were. Other hunters, seeing our tracks, probably thought there had been a stampede of wild animals through there and they would be right. He wanted the best deer stand spots for himself. This method also helped him to know if the tracks he saw next time were fresh ones.

When we got home Grandma would start to work on the Poke Sallet. It is a green leafy stalk that grows on roadsides and around freshly cleared areas. When it first sprouts up in the spring it is tender and kind of bites your tongue when you eat it boiled and then fried in a skillet with eggs scrambled in. Be advised though, that it is poisonous if not prepared properly. After washing it Grandma would boil it three times, each time pouring off the water and boiling it in fresh water. She would then fry it down in a black iron skillet with eggs, which scrambled and mixed in with the dark green Poke.

When the Poke Sallet was left to fully mature it had loads of deep purple berries. We were told never to eat them, but you could mash them to make a deep purple dye that stained anything it came in contact with. After a few helpings of Poke each spring, everyone's digestive systems were thoroughly purged and cleansed. As Grandpa put it, no one was bunged up after that. He might also add that one of the toddlers needed their hippin's (diapers) changed.

Chapter Thirteen

Dad Remembers the Hard Times

I suppose each generation thinks they had it worse than the young ones do now. I realize my ancestors had it a lot worse trying to raise their families than I did. My dad never let us forget it either. When we griped while we were working so hard in the big garden patch he always planted, he would tell us how deep the snow was when he used to walk to school for miles while barefoot. They didn't have much cash money so they bartered and traded with their neighbors and traveling peddlers. There were five children older than my Dad was and on the days he heard the peddler would be coming by, he would beat the others to the hens' nests and gather all the eggs he could find. He would trade the few eggs he found for candy, gum or firecrackers. I'm sure he was the spoiled one of the lot and gave Grandma many days of worry because he grew up to be quite the daredevil. She had to watch as he sped around on his motorcycle and later on he buzzed over the head of her cows flying a plane.

Dad was born during the Great Depression on October 9, 1927. During that time, if you could get a job you would have to work for very low wages. Each boy got one pair of brogan shoes and one pair of overalls each year. As the knees of the overalls wore out, Grandma would cut out the leg backs of some old overalls and sew them on the front legs that were thin and full of holes.

The Roberts family, at that time, lived about seven-and-a-half miles as a crow flies from the county seat of Sheridan, Arkansas. Grandpa would get up at four o'clock in the morning and walk that seven-and-a-half miles through the woods and work ten hours a day for ten cents per hour. He worked in a wagon yard ten hard hours for one dollar and then walked seven-and-a-half miles back home in the dark. Dad would be waiting for him at the end of the lane, which lead to the house. Even though he had been on his feet since four o'clock that morning, Dad could hear him still whistling as he walked the road home to his family.

When he had walked holes in the soles of his shoes, Grandpa would cut out pieces of old harness leather and put it in his shoes, only to wear it out again walking all those miles. No wonder he could still work rings around me when he was well into his eighties. Grandpa's younger life was spent in some heavy-duty aerobic activity. I still have the family's cobbler stand at my house. I believe some people call it a shoe last. It has a couple of sizes of iron feet that go on it. It is still attached to the original block of wood it has been on all these years. The children only got one pair of shoes a year. Most of the time they went barefoot, even when hunting, fishing or working the fields. Dad's feet were so tough when he went to the service, he won a lot of bets that he could strike a match on the bottom of his foot.

In late 1934 the Roberts family moved to a larger farm two miles northwest of Prattsville, Arkansas. This farm consisted of 160 acres of prime Saline River bottomland, the best in Grant County. It was owned by a man who was a buyer and trader of mules and horses. He would haul his unbroken mules and horses to the Roberts'. Grandpa and his four sons would train them and work them in the fields until there was a buyer for them. That is how they had enough stock to work the farm. In 1935, the first full year on this farm, they made 400 bushels of corn and 15 bales of cotton. Since they were sharecropping, the owner of the farm received 1/4 of the harvest for the use of his land. Cotton sold cheap that year. Dad told us of a song the old folks would sing. One verse went like this, "Eight cent cotton and forty cent meat, how in the hell can a poor man eat?"

When I was a child we were never allowed to sleep late, for Dad had been taught by Grandma and Grandpa that the early bird gets the worm. I have never been able to sleep late no matter when I go to bed. Childhood habits seem to have stuck with me. He would tell us how for six days a week they would get up at four a.m. Grandpa would go to the barn and feed the livestock and slop the hogs. When he got back to the house, Grandma had a hot, hardy breakfast waiting on the table. This went on for six days a week, Monday through Saturday. On Sunday morning Grandma would cook breakfast and dinner at the same time. She would then walk two miles to Sweet Home Church, taking as many children as possible with her. They always had a late dinner on Sunday.

Sometimes the pastor would eat with them. There wasn't any money to pay the pastor a salary so each family shared their crops and livestock with him. Periodically the pastor was given a pounding. No, this doesn't mean he was stoned to death. At a pounding the idea was for everyone to give the pastor one pound of whatever food they had available at that time. One pastor got such a large pounding, it is said his old car bumper was almost dragging the ground when he left for home.

Grandpa didn't go to church very often, but that didn't mean he wasn't a believer. Once he and Dad went squirrel hunting on Sunday. A limb fell out of a tree and hit Pa in the eye, almost blinding him. His conscience led him to believe it happened because he was hunting on Sunday. No more Sunday hunting for him!

He usually used Sunday morning time to mend fences or doctor sick or injured animals. Sometimes he would go to the barn and shell a sack of corn to be carried to the gristmill to be ground into corn meal for corn bread. About once a month it was Dad's job to ride a mule or a horse into Prattsville's gristmill with that sack of corn.

Grandpa would always tell Dad to walk the animal to and from the gristmill so the corn wouldn't spill, but as you know, boys will be boys.

He was riding a very spirited mule one day and when Dad kicked the mule in the side with his heel, Dad and the sack of corn ended up in a mud hole. The sack came untied and about half the corn was lost. He picked up all the corn he could and tried to catch the mule. The mule was spooked and ran all the way home and Dad got spooked by Grandpa when he arrived home with only half a sack of shelled corn and no meal.

If I asked for money to go to a movie, Dad would tell how he used to get his money for a Saturday night movie when he was my age. He would cut firewood for some neighbor or pick wild blackberries for 25 cents per gallon. One old gentleman would give him 50 cents to rake the chicken litter out from under his house. One uncle would give him 50 cents a day to help him cut and split fence post and build fences on his farm. After this Dad would say, "Have you ever heard the old saying, squeeze a nickel until the buffalo messes on himself?" If you ever asked for a free handout from Dad, you could count on a good story to back him up on his theory that nothing in his life was ever free.

The following is a good example of the reasoning behind his theory. Early one Saturday morning Grandpa had agreed to let Dad and his older brother Robert Lee use the wagon and a team of mules to haul firewood, which they were going to cut and haul for a neighbor. They were trying to make enough money for a trip to town that evening or maybe even a movie. They cut the load of wood with a crosscut saw and split it with an axe and maul. After it was stacked neatly in the neighbors' yard, they received one dollar and fifty cents.

Grandpa had one condition when he let them use the precious wagon. When they got back home they were to take it down the hill and put it in the creek so the water would soak and swell the wooden parts of the wheels, keeping the metal bands from falling off. In their haste to get off to town, these two eager boys forgot about this until after they had already unhooked the mules and turned them out to pasture. They came up with the bright idea that they could roll the wagon into the creek by hand.

Now this hill down to the creek was very steep and about thirty-five yards long. They pushed the wagon to the edge of the hill and used haywire to lock both back wheels, hoping to roll it slowly down the hill. They pushed it over the edge of the hill and everything was going just fine until about half way down, the haywire broke. The wagon went plunging on down the hill without the two boys and it didn't stop until the tongue of the wagon stuck in the creek bank and broke off.

Grandma showed up about that time and said, "You boys are in for it when your Papa gets here." She wouldn't let them go to town either. Well, Grandpa's temper being what it was and in this instance rightly so, he used a picket from the yard fence on the backside of his youngest. This gave Robert Lee enough time to decide he didn't want to stay around and he ran into the woods and didn't return until late that night. By that time Grandpa's temper had cooled off, so Robert Lee got off Scott free, according to his younger brother anyway.

On occasion, when they did earn enough money for a movie, they didn't have to go far in this rural community to see one. In Dad's day he could walk a mile up a gravel road where Mr. Gill, who it is said was an ex-carnival worker, had a movie theater set up in a tent. He had it fixed up as a real moneymaker. There were bleachers built inside so everyone, who paid their ten cents for a silent movie or fifteen cents for a talker, would be able to see.

Some, of course, would sneak in their home brew and end up falling off the top bleacher. Mr. Gill also had a monkey who kept everyone entertained as well as those who drank too much brew. There was also another gentleman in the community who had a monkey. Mr. Nance ran the store across from the Roberts home. In the summer, maybe on the 4th of July, he would hold a carnival in the large, open field across from the store. Dad told us how Mr. Nance would call out in a shrill voice for people to stop and see the monkey climb the pole.

There was a young man who courted a young lady who lived nearby the Roberts family. This guy would borrow his Dad's truck, which had a canvas cover over the back, to pick up his date. To pay for his dates and gas for the truck, he would pick up anyone who was waiting at the store and take them to the Movie Theater in Sheridan for five cents round trip. A smooth two bits were needed before a guy could think about making this trip and having enough to get into the theater, never mind any refreshment or taking a date. I don't remember the Movie Theater, but I do remember seeing a couple of movies at the Sheridan Drive-In Movies. It is sad to say both of those entertainment establishments are long gone.

It was very important to Dad that all his children get a high school education. He said his own schooling came up a bit short. He attended his first six years of school, which went pretty well, at Sweet Home Elementary School. This building was later converted to a residence and it still stands across the road from Sweet Home Church. At that time each community had their own elementary or one-room schools and after 6th grade you had to move on to Prattsville High. There were several of these small community schools: Sweet Home, Liberty, Davis Creek, Paxton, and Dogwood to name a few. When Dad had to go to Prattsville High School, he said he didn't fare well with all those city children and anyway Grandpa needed him to help out on the farm, so that was the end of his formal education.

By this time Dad's two oldest brothers had left the farm and gotten themselves better jobs. That left Grandpa, two sons, Grandma and two daughters to work the farm and harvest the results. About 1940 Grandpa bought the farm they had been working for $2100 dollars and sold it in 1941 for $2500 dollars. They moved to the next farm north up river. This farm consisted of 180 acres and was owned by a lawyer. It was not very good for row crops so they bought a few cattle and tried a bit of ranching, which didn't work out. It was too much land for a man and one son to work. The older boys had been drafted into the army at the beginning of World War II and both daughters were married and gone from home.

In 1943, with the help of their oldest son who was in the army, the Roberts bought a small place right on the Sal Burnett Pike, not far from Murl Cline hill. There was 20 acres, which was just enough for a garden and pasture for Grandma's two milk cows Pet and Brindle. It was very convenient for them because it was across the road from the store and just a stone's throw through the woods to the church. Grandpa and Dad both got jobs cutting logs with a cross cut saw. They made more cash money cutting timber than they had at farming.

Then, they received word that the oldest son, Frank had been severely wounded in battle. He was sent to England 78th General Hospital where his brother Calvin worked as a ward medic, so they got to visit often. This along with Grandma's prayers are what probably kept him alive so he would finally return to the states. Frank was later sent to LaGrange Army Hospital in New Orleans. When he was put in the plane on a gurney, he was amazed to meet another hometown soldier on the same plane.

Frank sent money home so someone could come to see him. Well, Grandma was who he wanted to see, I'm sure, but she was no traveler. So my Dad, Bennie Ray, at the age of 17 was given the chance of a lifetime. Having never been out of the state of Arkansas and probably not even out of Grant County very far, he was put on a bus to, of all places, New Orleans.

It was 1944 and the bus to New Orleans was crowded as well as the streetcars of New Orleans. Dad said he got to know Canal Street very well because the Army hospital was on one end of Canal St. and where he was staying was on the other end. I wonder how he felt working barefoot in the dirt one day and having to wear shoes and his Sunday best to take in the sites of the world between here and Canal Street?

Although I'm sure Uncle Frank would have preferred to have his loving, nurturing mother at his side, rather than this 17-year-old green, gawky, country boy, he probably figured his money was well spent. After all this Uncle Frank did pull through and received many years of nurturing from his mother.

It wasn't long after this that the young Bennie was himself drafted and again Grandma had to say goodbye to one of her sons. At least when he left this time, he was already a little wise to the ways of the world, for after all, he had made it to New Orleans and back by himself.

Chapter Fourteen

Wedding Bells

Dad was discharged from the army in early 1950 and after meeting my Mom, who was nine years younger, married her that fall. They will celebrate their golden wedding anniversary this year, October 9, 2000 as well as Dad's birthday. Yes, he will never forget getting a fourteen-year-old bride on his twenty-third birthday. What a fuss that would create today if Mom's fourteen-year-old granddaughter married a twenty-three-year-old. Mom still says she was a lot more mature then than the teenagers are now.

If she wasn't grown up when she married, she had to grow up fast. She had a lot to learn and Grandma was willing to teach her young daughter-in-law how a country wife took care of their family properly. Mom was a good student. She can still out cook, out clean, and stretch money better than anyone else I know.

She had to have been good at being a homemaker and a mother; after all she raised me, didn't she? My Mom deserves any modern convenience that exists. She certainly didn't have any during the first years of her young married life.

The couples that marry now split up at the first sign of inconvenience or trouble. I'm sure it wasn't easy for my parents, but I am certainly proud of the fact that they are still together after fifty years. It was my privilege to open my home to so many of their friends and family for their golden anniversary celebration. To see them able to be up and dance to a love song was a thrill, I'll never forget.

I am sure their grandchildren and great-grandchildren won't either. They were amazed that Mam-maw and Papaw could still remember how to keep time with the music and they didn't even step on each other's toes. I told the girls, don't let that white hair fool you, Mam-maw still has more spunk than any of the rest of us do.

Chapter Fifteen

Oregon, Here We Come, Again and Again and Again!

Jobs were not plentiful in Arkansas in the early '50s. Dad and my uncle were working for the Arkansas Highway Department for 67 cents per hour. This was not enough to pay the rent and feed their wife and babies. They were on a crew, which spread pea gravel on hot asphalt. When the temperature hit the high 90s, their feet would blister through the soles of their shoes.

My uncle said there had to be a better way and place to make a living. Dad agreed wholeheartedly and they quit, not knowing where they would go next. They had a good friend in Oregon who they called and asked about work on the West Coast. It seemed all the sawmills and timber-cutting crews were hiring every day and were paying $2.00 per hour and up depending on experience. He could have a job lined up for them, but the catch was they had to be in Oregon within a week.

They didn't have enough money to make the trip, but Dad had a 1948 Ford car, which had been wrecked, and he had the title to it. The Grant County Bank in Sheridan loaned him $300.00 on the title of said wrecked vehicle. The money was to be paid back at $50.00 per month with interest. They left for Oregon that same day, each leaving a wife and new baby girl at home in Arkansas.

While they were driving through Little Rock, Arkansas in a 1940 Studebaker, the transmission locked in high gear. When they stopped at a red light, my uncle would slip the clutch to get the car moving. They continued to ride the clutch all the way to Arizona. Once when they stopped in Flagstaff, Arizona at a red light on a steep hill, the Studebaker just couldn't get going. The clutch was smoking and stinking.

Snow was about two feet deep on the highway. Dad got out and crawled under the car far enough that he could use a hammer to knock the shift lever into second gear. They stayed in that gear until they got out of town. Somewhere along the way, a spring hanger broke under the car and the frame dropped down on the tires. They jacked the car up and put a fence post between the axle and the frame. Their next stop was a junkyard where they purchased a used spring hanger.

After that everything went well until they got to the mountains of northern California and southern Oregon.

The faithful little old Studebaker started getting hot and losing power on the mountains, so Dad would have to crawl under the car and use the hammer on the shift lever again. His estimate of his doing this was at least fifty times before they arrived in Oregon. By this time they were running short of money and of all things the generator went out on the car. Not having enough money for a new one meant they had to travel during the day and have the battery charged at night.

On the seventh day, they made it to their friends' house in Oregon. Sure enough, Dad went to work that very night at Wilbur Lumber Company Saw Mill for $2.00 per hour. Their friends let them stay at their house for three weeks, until they got a payday and a place to stay. Herschel and Madora Hollinger will never be forgotten for their good deed.

After about six weeks they sent home money so their wives and babies could come to Oregon by train. I was three months old when my young skinny Mom and her equally skinny sister set off to Oregon with their two baby girls. What a trip that must have been. From my baby pictures, anyone can see I was a heavy load to bear. But, all bragging aside, I was a beautiful baby and Mom seemed to get a lot of help from some GI's who were on the train.

One GI in particular helped Mom a great deal with me. I'm sure she must have appreciated any help she could get on that long trip. She was surprised though, when Dad and my uncle met the train at a stop where she was supposed to have a long layover. It is my understanding that Mom didn't recognize him at first because he had grown a red beard for some type of frontier festival. She recognized the voice though when he asked whom that man was holding his baby. The GI said goodbye and stated he would like to see me when I grew up. Wouldn't it be a shock if he could see me now?

The Arkansas migrants would work from four-and-a-half months to six months depending on the Oregon weather and then the caravan back to Arkansas would form. Once back home, they would usually hunt and draw unemployment through the winter. In early spring we would be back on our way to Oregon.

We weren't the only family who did this migration every spring. Most of the whole community did this for several years in a row. The second year, Dad got two jobs: one falling timber in the daytime and the other working at a plywood mill at night. He did this for about two months until he had trouble staying awake and he quit the plywood mill.

In later years, if I ever griped about the lack of space or privacy in our home, I was told about the primitive lodgings that my Mom had to endure as a young mother in Oregon.

The migrants from Arkansas would try to congregate in either the homemade trailers at the Hansen's place or the Harvey cabins. Mom's whole house consisted of a small one-room trailer with one bed and a hot plate for cooking and a young baby (me). There was a shower house and laundry room for all to share in the middle of the trailers.

Of course these were wringer washers and tubs for rinsing.

There were no automatic dryers here; everything was hung on the clothesline, a practice that my Mom still does today in nice weather. Try it sometime; your sheets will smell a lot fresher. Mom managed better than I would have, for she not only existed in this environment day to day, but she also cooked for unexpected company. All she had to cook on was a hot plate and somehow she would even find them a place to sleep.

My Mom was one gutsy lady then and what a survivor. I've decided I must have been a model baby for her to be able to do what she did with so little. She and Dad both have said there was no end to the willing babysitters that wanted to keep me if they went hunting or whatever.

On one trip to Oregon, they bought a three-room house that sat in their friend's front yard. The only stipulation was that the house had to be moved. Mr. Crystal, Dad's boss, had a bulldozer brought in and some huge logs. The house was jacked up and skidded up the hill on those logs.

Mom now had more room, but she still spent a good deal of time and energy carrying water up that hill and probably with me on one hip. She furnished her new home with furniture and things she bought at auctions. A few of those items were brought back to Arkansas, but most were left for the new owners of the little house in Wilbur, Oregon.

There was one hunting trip the guys had planned up in the mountains and the wives all decided they wouldn't be left behind. Thank goodness they left me with someone this time. All of the vehicles took off for the mountains with mattresses tied on top and loaded to the top with cooking gear and blankets, but no tents. The campsite must have looked like a wagon train with all of those mattresses in a circle and a cooking fire in the middle.

Much to their surprise the next morning, everyone was completely covered in snow. The snow had actually kept them warmer. The hunt was very successful, so the men were reluctant to leave. Mom had promised to be back for me on a certain day, but evidently none of the men were worried about that.

I can just see her saying well, I'll go by myself then. Another lady said she would go with her. Those silly men loaded a deer on each front fender of the Studebaker and one on the trunk and off the two young women went in the middle of the night down that icy, snow-covered mountain. They made it home in the wee hours of the morning and feasted on scrambled eggs and Vienna sausages. Where did she get that much gumption? I have a stubborn streak, but my cowardice outweighs my stubborn streak.

On one trip home from Oregon we rode with my aunt and uncle and their three daughters. This was a total of four adults and four children in one vehicle. My uncle had just had all his teeth pulled and was unable to drive. I was teething and he said he would take care of me if Mom and Dad would do the driving.

At some point one night I ended up in the front seat between Dad and Aunt Millie. Dad was speeding and the officer who pulled us over had a glowing nightstick. Dad said all the time the policeman was trying to write a ticket, I was jabbering and reaching out the window for that light. He finally let me play with it and forgot about the ticket. Where did I lose all that innocent charm?

One trip Dad made to Oregon, Mom was expecting again, so we stayed in Malvern across the street from my Grandma Etta. Just after my brother was born, I was stricken with polio and had to have around-the-clock care. I remember trying to escape from the two doctors who made house calls even though I was between two and three years old.

There are also memories of my Dad and others giving me alcohol baths and my seeing people and other children staring at me through the windows. God blessed me and I don't have any disabilities that a lot of people have from that epidemic.

It was time for us to go to Oregon again and Mr. Crystal had already wired Dad the money for us to finance the trip, when tragedy again struck. Dad's older brother, Robert Lee, was hit by a car and killed. Dad couldn't leave Grandma just then, so he sent the money back to Oregon and that was the end of our migration trips there. We moved in with Grandma and Grandpa for a while, I guess to help them over their loss.

Chapter Sixteen

Remember the Wakes and Who They Were For

This is again one of those times that I was so young that I can only remember bits and pieces. About the only thing I can remember of Robert Lee is that he sat me on top of a black horse once. When his body lay in state in that little living room, I vaguely remember someone trying to keep me from that area. I thought it was my daddy because they looked so much alike.

The tradition of bringing the body of one's dead home for a few days and nights so you could have a wake is pretty much non-existent now. Everyone would sit up with the body and drink coffee to stay awake. There would be an over abundance of food brought in by friends and neighbors. I think in times like this everyone feels helpless, and bringing the food is a way to feel as though you are doing something, even though you know there is nothing anyone can do to make the grieving family feel any differently.

I don't know if someone requested it, if a funeral home would accommodate this request now or not. Grandmother's body was brought home in 1966 for a wake. By that time, I had been introduced to this tradition many times, but it was still hard because I felt guilty for not spending her last days with her and now it was too late to tell her what I wanted to.

By the time Grandpa died there was no discussion about bringing his body home to lie in state. It was just understood that the wake would be at the funeral home. Having felt so guilty when my grandmothers died, I guess my lesson had been learned and I tried making it up by spending more time with Grandpa during his last days.

Even though he went to a nursing home, which broke all our hearts, we tried to see he was taken care of. He was a man of very few words when he had gotten well into his nineties. I had never heard him say please or thank you for anything.

I'll never forget the last words he spoke to me. He was completely bedfast then because he had broken a hip. I always made sure to get him to drink some water when I visited. This particular day, he kept saying he was cold. One of Grandma's hand pieced quilts had been taken to the nursing home with him. When I got it out of the closet and covered him with it, to my amazement he said thank you! After a quick kiss on his cheek, I had to get out of that place.

The next time we saw each other was in a hospital emergency room and it was too late to talk to him again. He was taken to intensive care where a room full of our family was able to be with him for the short time it took for him to take his last breath here on this earth. I just wish I had been able to be there for Grandma too.

Thinking back at Grandpa now, I have many fond memories and there are so many small things everyone in Sweet Home still tells about him. One such story that is repeated over and over is the one when he wrestled with a huge catfish in the river.

He and the boys had some set hooks set out in Saline River. One morning it was raining cats and dogs and Pa told the boys to stay in bed and he would go to the river alone. When he approached one of the set hooks, he knew he had something big caught because the tree the hook was tied to was bent in the water and there was a lot of thrashing about.

Well, it could have been one of the huge loggerhead turtles he sometimes caught, but it wasn't. Just about the time he reached out and caught the line, he saw it was a humongous catfish. At the same time the tree branch broke and his feet slipped out from under him. He landed on the catfish and the wrestling match was on. The fish was slippery and I guess a better swimmer than Pa so all he had when he got home was one fantastic tale.

Either this tale was true or he had to have an excuse for being so muddy and falling in the river. Either way, this fish story was believed by all and is still repeated today. It is not out of the realm of possibility, for there were huge catfish in the river then. They would feed a lot of people and still Grandma would can some of the catfish right along with buffalo fish and red horse fish.

Chapter Seventeen

Duck Hunting You Say!

Have you ever heard a story that you could just picture in your mind and wish you had been there to see it? Well, I have heard one that probably made Dad and two of his friends look like the Three Stooges.

They had gone to the river and put one of the guy's homemade wooden boats in the river so they could duck hunt. They had been successful in bagging several ducks, when they rounded a bend in the river and there on the bank was a group of hogs. Without any thought as to how they would ever get one of these monstrosities home, one of the stooges fired a successful shot and down went the biggest hog of all of them.

They knew they couldn't possibly lift the hog high enough to put it in the boat without overturning it. They used their belts and vines to drag the hog as close to the water as possible. The owner of the boat motored to where the bank hung over the water. The idea was for the two on the bank to slowly lower the hog into the boat.

Just as they were trying to lower it, the vines broke and the hog landed in the boat all right. The only thing was that the boat, hog and man all went under. The hog finally started to float to the top, allowing the boat to rise some. They had to find anything they could to dip water out of the boat and finally succeeded in raising it all the way.

They now realized they were way out in the woods with a freshly killed hog and there was no way that hog and three men were going to be able to ride in that boat together. There was one possibility, if they beheaded it and gutted it right there on the spot, perhaps they could make it.

They made it, with no room to spare. The water was within a couple of inches of spilling into the boat as they slowly made their way back home. Everyone joked about their going duck hunting and coming back with more pork than ducks.

Chapter Eighteen

Tight Wad Times

If you heard of a community called Tight Wad, you might think everyone who lived there was a miser. However, that isn't the origin of that name. It is called that because the road in that area creates a circle in which the houses are close together. They weren't as close in the city sense, but they were unusually close for country standards. There was only one way in and one way out so everyone knew when a stranger was in the area.

We migrated to Oregon for three years in a row until Mom and Dad had another child and they had saved enough money to buy a small place here in Tight Wad, Arkansas. It consisted of three rooms and a path. This three-room tarpaper house became a haven for those who still migrated back and forth to Oregon.

When someone needed a place to stay, Mom made Baptist pallets on the floor for us kids. Dad worked in a mine for a while and had access to wooden dynamite boxes. These dynamite boxes were nailed on the kitchen walls and used for sitting at the eating table. We lived in this house until I was sixteen years old.

There was a great amount of improvements and rooms added through the years. Dad and Mom tore down an old house and used the lumber to build us a girl's and boy's bedroom and also added an indoor bath.

Grandma papered our rooms over the beaded boards. The girl's room had roses on the wall and the boy's had cowboys and Indians. It wasn't long before the wallpaper cracked because of the beaded board behind it. This house still has more good memories for me than the one we moved to later. I guess it is because I lived longer there, than where my parents live today which is only about two miles from the old house.

Many things come to my mind when I think of our years in Tight Wad. Once Dad and I went to a dairy in Sheridan to get a calf we could raise on a bottle. He thought we could fatten it up and butcher it for meat. I really don't recall him butchering any of the calves we raised. We kids put up such a fuss that I think he just sold them.

What was funny was the fact that we didn't have a truck, so Dad improvised and took the back seat out of the old car. Not only did we come home with a calf in the car, but a dog also. The man who owned the dairy offered me a collie dog. I thought that dog was prettier and smarter than Lassie and of course Dad put her in the car with the calf and home we went.

We named that dog Lady and she was a member of the family for many years. She didn't act very much like a Lady when Mom or Dad tried to punish one of us. She could become downright nasty when trying to protect us kids. She also hated snakes and saved us several times from stepping on a rattlesnake and getting bitten.

I can't ever remember us not having a dog or some kind of pet. The only cats we were allowed were the ones at Grandma's and Dad made us leave them there. Once we had a dog named Trixie who looked like the Pete on Little Rascals. She had several litters of puppies, but one litter met a tragic death. They fell in a hole into the well and that meant we had to haul water again. Dad had to fish the puppies out and disinfect the well. Needless to say, we kids were very upset.

That well eventually went dry and Dad had to dig another one. If you have never seen a well being dug by hand, you can't imagine what hard work it is.

First of all, he had an old man witch (some people call it douse) for a water vein. He took a forked stick and held it in his hands with the stick pointing out level in front of him. When he got over a vein of underground water, the stick would bend to the ground even though he had a firm grip on the forked ends.

The only good vein he could detect was a good distance out in the field behind the house. Since Dad had a lot of faith in the old-timer, that is where they started to dig. They made a huge wooden windless kind of like a huge spool with handles on it. They put it over the spot where they were going to dig and wrapped a big heavy rope around the spool of the windless. Using a pick and shovel they started to dig, taking turns trying to shovel the hard ground. When the hole got over their head, a bucket was tied to the end of the rope and one of the guys helping would sit on the bucket and the others would lower him into the hole using the windless. When he had dug a bucket full of dirt, they would winch it up and empty it and send it back down to be filled up again.

This hole was only thirty-six inches in diameter, so a very big man couldn't go down into the hole and have room to dig. They dug and dug for several days and nights until they hit the good vein of water that the witching stick detected. They then lowered concrete well tiles down into the hole to keep the sides from caving in.

How thankful we were that we now had plenty of water and didn't have to be saving with it. Even though it had to be piped a long way that was better than hauling enough water for six people.

That old water witcher is dead now. My husband is now witching wells for people. Not everyone can do it and I don't know how it works but it does. People from all around here have called on him to witch a well for them. He can also straighten out a couple of clothes hangers and use them to find utility lines that are underground. When he ran a backhoe, he kept a set of these wires with him so he could locate the lines and not dig into them.

Sometimes I wonder how my mischievous brothers ever survived their childhood. One of them fell out of a moving vehicle twice. Mom made a U-turn in front of the store and she didn't miss him until she looked in the rear view mirror and saw people running to pick him up out of the highway. He escaped without a scratch. The other time he was older and when we made a turn in the old truck he was leaning against the door. Well, the door swung open and he held onto the door until we could get stopped.

Once when they were very small I thought they weren't going to survive Dad's wrath. They were playing service station and they played like they were servicing Dad's car. They filled the tank all right, with sand. Every time Dad tried to drive that car with it spitting and sputtering, he got mad at the boys all over again.

We had the whole neighborhood looking for Eddie one day. He was missing for quite awhile, that is until he woke from his nap. He had taken an old army duffel bag and climbed into the back of our truck. That ornery boy got into the duffel bag and pulled the drawstring up tight, ignored us calling for him and went to sleep. When he woke up he loosened the drawstring and crawled out wondering what all the excitement was about.

I wasn't an angel either. In elementary school we had an elderly teacher who was known to throw things at students and even spanked them sometimes for no valid reason. So naturally I was scared when, in the third grade, another student was going to tell on me for accidentally hitting another kid with a ball, which she failed to catch. I was so scared I ran away from school.

I was well on my way home when I saw the teacher's car in the distance. Quickly I crawled under the barbwire fence and hid behind a pond levee. When she passed me and was out of sight, I crawled out and started walking home again. This was a distance of over three miles that I planned to walk. I was saved when some ladies from our community picked me up and took me safely home, or so I thought.

When we got there, I only had time to run in the house and scream for Momma, when the teacher drove up. All Mom could get out of me was that the teacher was going to whip me. Well, that wasn't going to happen until Mom heard both sides of the story.

The teacher's mind was set to whip me and take me back to school. Both of their tempers flared and in the end the teacher was back in her car backing out the driveway with Mom trying to get the car door open. While the teacher didn't get to paddle me, I do remember Dad put his belt across my behind a couple of times, but that was so much better than getting whipped in front of everyone at school.

It just so happened that some carpenters were working on our house that day. One of the men ended up being my father-in-law and as long as he was alive, he never let me forget that day I ran away from school.

Probably twenty-five years later while working in a hospital, I saw that my old teacher was a patient. Curiosity got the best of me and I just had to see if it really was her. Well, it was and she seemed so glad to see one of her former students all grown up and married. But to my surprise, she got very serious and emotional when she apologized for her erratic behavior. She stated she had been too old to teach that year and she should have quit long before she did.

When I was in elementary school, a lot of the kids were taking piano lessons from a teacher who came to the school. Without a piano to practice on, there was no sense in my taking lessons. A man with a piano in the back of his truck came by the station where Dad worked one day. That night when Dad came in I had gained a piano and Dad had lost a chainsaw. I wish I still had that piano. It was a beautiful old upright with a lot of carving and detail on it.

I took lessons for about three years and even played in one recital. I'll never forget the teacher giving me a choice of playing either Brahm's Lullaby or Little Birdie in a Tree. I chose the latter because if I goofed no one would know the difference, but everyone knows how Brahm's Lullaby sounds. I dearly loved my teacher, Mrs. Lewis.

When she remarked how she liked a dress I wore, it became my usual dress to wear on music days. My other grandmother had made it for me out of a material that had roses all over it. After Mrs. Lewis left, I couldn't seem to get interested in the lessons anymore and ended up quitting.

Now I wish my parents had forced the issue, but instead they sold the piano. Now I have a piano in my home but still can't play.

Most of the families in Tight Wad had numerous children. We could fill the school bus full by the time it went around the loop. All of the children got along well, so I don't recall any of us quarreling. We stuck together. I wish I had a dollar for every time I rode my bike around that gravel loop of a road.

Once I was doubling my sister who was probably about three at the time. My bike was a blue Western Flyer with a light on front and a flat rack on the back for a passenger to sit on. I was zipping around the loop with my sister Belva on the back. She must have gotten tired of holding her legs out away from the wheel. Well, she dropped her bare feet and one went right into the wheel spokes cutting her heel almost completely off. Needless to say the bike stopped suddenly and almost dumped me off.

The neighbors heard my screams and helped get us home and then the injured one to the doctor. I felt guilty and scared that she would lose her foot and I was responsible. It wasn't as bad as I feared, but she had stitches and bandages for quite some time and had to be coaxed to walk again. She may have enjoyed my carrying her around on my hip.

Tight Wad, Arkansas is located approximately one mile from Sweet Home. The ladies of these communities were as close as the kids were. At one time they had a Birthday Club. When someone had a birthday, everyone brought a dish for potluck and a gift to that lady's home.

The honoree was supposed to have something planned that she needed done.

Sometimes they quilted her quilt she had pieced. Sometimes they cleaned, painted or canned. But most of all they had a good day of visiting and maybe a little gossiping. They didn't dare miss their soap opera, "As The World Turns" on that day either. It was pretty much a clean family show then. Television has sure changed since then.

At one time there were three grocery stores in these two communities. They all were gathering places for gossip and one usually had a table of women playing canasta. Sometimes there would be a domino game going on also. For a while, our neighborhood barber was located in the feed room of one store. She was a self-taught haircutter who talked nonstop and that was okay because she couldn't hear you talk unless you hollered at the top of your lungs.

It didn't matter where she moved in the community; her business followed her. People paid her what they wanted to. I remember some people paying twenty-five cents and some were more generous.

She still has a little home in the community but she resides in a nursing home. There are a lot of men who miss her haircuts and being able to catch up on the news while sitting in her barber chair. She also plucked and shaped ladies' eyebrows and dyed them. I have watched her do my Mom's many times. These talents made her a living for many, many years.

On our way to Grandma's, we would pick up coke bottles and return them to the store for spending money. We only got a few cents for each bottle, but it would be enough to get some penny candy. If we had a good bottle haul, we could get a candy bar and a Coke. We had to be careful buying candy bars at one store because sometimes you might find a worm. You sure didn't take a bite until you had examined it very well.

My oldest brother was nicknamed Scrooge because he would not spend his money. I still call him Scrooge, even though he has gotten over being so tight-fisted with his money. He would ask for a bite of my candy bar and nearly devour the whole thing in one bite. Then he would ask my little brother for a drink of his Coke and he would gulp it all down.

One of our favorite treats was to get a package of peanuts and put them in our Coke and we would get a few nuts with each drink.

Scrooge also sold Grit papers around the neighborhood. It was a favorite for many of the ladies because they could order sewing patterns from it, get new recipes as well as reading the odd stories the paper contained.

There were many other ways we made spending money. The farmers in the area could drive around the loop and pick up a truckload of kids to haul hay. In the winter when Mr. Tom needed us to help at his chicken farm, we all jumped right in those chicken houses, running around catching chickens and holding a good grip on their legs. When you had at least two in each hand, you would hand them up to someone on the truck who would put them in wooden crates. The next stop for those chickens was the soup factory. Then the houses had to be cleared of the chicken litter and later they would be restocked with fresh laying hens.

My classmates and I got the chicken-catching job in two counties. Sometimes the chickens were in small cages, several in one cage. You had to reach in and grab their legs and pull them out of the small cage door. We also hauled hay, chicken litter, cow manure and held car washes to pay for our senior trip to Houston & Galveston.

When we caught chickens, we wouldn't get home until the wee hours of the morning, stinking of chicken litter and feathers stuck all over us. By the time you stripped, bathed and washed your hair it was almost time to be at school.

Once a carload of us was on our way home from an all night chicken chase. Being very hungry, we stopped where they had carhops to take your order. We sure couldn't go in anywhere to eat. When the carhop stuck her head up to the car window, she drew back suddenly and we knew she had gotten a good whiff of our odor. We couldn't smell ourselves because our nostrils were full of the stench of dead chickens, feathers and litter. We got our food okay, but we knew she hated to come close to that car again. Needless to say we didn't care if we ever had chicken noodle soup or fried chicken again.

After school in the afternoons, Tight Wad was a busy place. You could bet there was some type of ball game going on in someone's yard. At our house we usually played basketball or football. Softball was the game of choice when we were in some of the other yards. We also had a tire swing or bag swing hanging from our big oak tree. We loved to see who could swing the highest.

One summer when I was about 13, Dad decided there were more than enough boys in the same age range to organize a baseball team. Our neighbor offered his field between our house and his for a ball field. Dad bought the necessary equipment, including a catcher's mitt, facemask, and padding, for his Tight Wad team. We built a backstop in that cow pasture full of bitter weeds. The only competition they had was another group of boys of all ages from another community.

Dad had to be out of town a lot, so in his absence, I was the one who practiced the boys. I didn't get to play in the games, but they let me keep the score. These boys knew not to cross me, because they had seen what I did to corral one of my brothers once.

I was left in charge at home one day. All the boys were at our house planning a trip to the woods to build a tree house. Well I was supposed to make sure all four of us kids were home when our parents came in. Scrooge thought he would just slide on out the door behind his buddies. I caught him by the collar as he was going out the door and landed one lucky punch right smack in his nose. Blood immediately squirted out his nose and down his shirt. The boys went to the woods without Scrooge that day. He is over 40 years old now and remembers that bloody nose vividly.

When it was time for the team to play at our opponent's field, Dad would drive around the loop and all the boys would climb in the back of our old faded red, 57 Chevy pickup that had cattle racks on the bed. It probably looked like a cage full of monkeys when we went through Sheridan with all those boys hanging on the cattle racks. Most of them had nicknames like Scrooge, Pudge and Slewfoot.

We were a close-knit neighborhood and everyone trusted each other. When I was sent to Mr. Tom's for eggs, I would just get a flat of eggs and write it on his calendar. We would pay up on payday. When we went to the dairy for milk, each gallon was written on their calendar. We had the first and only phone in Tight Wad for a while. Mom had a calendar hanging above the phone so any of our neighbors could write down their long distance phone calls.

At one time or another we had a grocery bill at all three of the community stores and sometime at the store in Prattsville also. Everyone charged in those days, not with a credit card, but the grocer kept a ticket book for each family. At one of the stores we could get a free ice cream cone or Coke when Mom paid the bill. That was the same store where there was usually a group of ladies playing canasta or maybe men playing dominoes or Rook. We miss the small community stores because they are all closed now.

It wasn't uncommon for our house to be used for jam sessions by several local musicians. Our home was not large by any means, but the furniture very often was moved out of the living room to make room for drums and guitars along with the old piano before it was sold. Corn meal sometimes was poured on the old wood floor to make it easier to do anything from the jitterbug to the twist. Not one of these musicians made the big time, but they sure had fun trying. It is fun to look at the old pictures from that era and see how everyone was enjoying themselves while drinking nothing stronger than Coke or coffee. This group of musicians sometimes volunteered their time to play at the local mental institution for the patients' Thursday night dance. The musicians performed from a stage while we looked down from the balcony to watch the patients dance. You could tell this was the highlight of their week and they dressed up in the finest they had to come to the dance.

Chapter Nineteen

On Top of Ole Smokey

Sometime later Dad and his brother bought a farm about three miles north of our home. They invested in a small herd of cows. It was on this farm that we kids all learned to drive. It was a necessity for us to be able to drive the hay trucks in the summer. At that time everyone baled their hay in rectangle-shaped, smaller bales than the huge round ones of today. The smaller kids drove the trucks while the larger ones would run along picking up the bales and tossing them on the truck so the one on the truck could stack them tightly.

More than one person was thrown from the back of the truck when the young driver couldn't get the hang of using the clutch. I wonder how many kids today would know how to start a vehicle pushing a button on the dash, with your left foot on the clutch and your right foot on the starter pedal? Some of them wouldn't even know how to dim the lights on our old truck we still have that has a dimmer button on the floor.

Hay hauling time was always hot and the hay made you itch. A trip to the river after this hot task was finished, was always in order. The farm was a lot of work. There was always some fence to build or chicken fertilizer to spread over the huge garden spots Dad always planted. We kids always swore we would never eat any purple hull peas or corn if he would just not make us pick those long rows. Of course that strategy never worked.

One year he had a huge watermelon patch and I learned that a lot of my school buddies used to love to raid it in the middle of the night. I was out of high school before they brought this fact to my attention. Even though we had watermelons, my brothers and their friends loved to raid another man's patch. He followed their half-eaten evidence right to them after one of these raids and they had to pay for their being so mischievous.

With this farm we inherited a crudely built deer camp called Ole Smokey. It consisted of two rooms, which were framed with wooden bark covered poles harvested from the land. It was covered with tin that had been painted light green. The front door had a wooden latch, which you opened by pulling a string to raise the latch on the inside. In one end of the front room was a huge wood cook stove. In the middle was a table at least ten feet long with a church bench behind it and wooden chairs around the rest. In the other end was a couch and a stove made out of a barrel to use for heat. The back room consisted of as many beds as it would hold. I remember at least four double beds and an old hospital bed for me.

Water was carried uphill in buckets from a spring that flowed out of a hillside out back. There was also a path to the outside john. We had a footbridge over a large, deep gully so the guys could get to their dogs in the pen. There was a gas-powered generator to use at night for lights. Earlier we used Coleman lanterns and kerosene lamps for light.

Before deer season, Mom would stock the camp with groceries and then the men would divide up the grocery bill. I remember she always bought a full stick of bologna and a full side of bacon. She had to buy lots of flour, because she mixed her breakfast biscuits in a dishpan every morning before daylight. She never knew how many she would have to feed that day. She didn't just feed the campers, but any hunter who decided they wanted to drop by for one of the three meals a day she cooked. There was a kitty can placed in sight; some contributed to the expense of their meal or coffee and some did not.

At night there was always card playing, story swapping and lots of joking going on. Usually we kids were sent to bed early because we had to go to school. Sometimes our homemade camper was our sleeping room, so we would be out of the noise and could sleep.

This camp building became in danger of sliding down into the deep gully, so a new one was constructed a little closer to the road. The wood stove did not make it to the new one. We now had a propane refrigerator and the cabinet sported a new red water pump. It was hand operated but still easier than carrying all those buckets of water up the hill. Mom had a propane cook stove with four regular burners and a large one in the middle where she kept a huge pan of water heating or a pot of mulligan stew. The long table and barrel stove were still used, but there was now a sectional sofa that wrapped around the barrel stove.

About that time several hunters who were of the same family decided to start their own deer camp. I guess we had outgrown our little cabin even though another sleeping quarters had been built for younger couples.

Deer camps covered this area and the names have survived all these years. There was one called Spit and Argue. After awhile, Spit and Argue split into two camps. Two sisters with gray hair started their own, which was called Spit and Spraddle since it was for ladies. I suppose they must have dipped snuff and the rest is self-explanatory. Spit and Spraddle was on the corner where we turned to get to Ole Smokey. Later came Big John, named after one of our dogs that loved to visit there. After that there was one called Wino's. The newest ones are just simply named after the families who camp there. It isn't as much fun for the hunters now because you have to join a lease and all the roads have locked gates on them.

Our deer camp was disbanded and all of us kids have used the cabin at one time or another over the years to have a temporary roof over our heads. It has been moved further off the road now and stands unoccupied for the first time in its history. The first time I lived in it there still was no electricity, no bathroom, and we still used the hand pump for water. The second time we lived in it while we were building our house, we added electricity and a bathroom.

Chapter Twenty

Deer Days in Arkansas

In most areas of the country you can tell fall is just around the corner when the leaves begin to change to golden yellows, deep reds or bright orange. The Sweet Home area went by a totally different sign. Usually around the beginning of October, every male who could coax even the sparsest beard to grow did so. There didn't seem to be any rhyme or reason for it, just a macho tradition, I guess. At church you saw them comparing their beards to everyone else's. They did this in preparation for deer season, which began in November. Everything totally revolved around deer season. Those who had vacation time from work took it then. Those who didn't usually managed to change their shift or to get laid off from work so they could hunt. The first day of the season was scheduled as a legitimate holiday at all schools in the county. Every man, woman and child was affected by deer season in some form or fashion. One young boy at church was asked if he knew the four seasons. He proudly stated yes, squirrel season, deer season, turkey season, and rabbit season. In anticipation of the season, all deer dogs had to be trained and practiced well in advance.

We kids spent many nights in the car listening to the dogs trail and run deer. You weren't allowed to talk because the men couldn't hear the dogs well enough to tell whose dog jumped the deer or was in the lead. I don't know how they thought they could tell if it was Jack or Jill, Lonesome or Queen, Big John or Colonel, Popcorn or Blue.

These dogs would not be allowed as hunting dogs today, because they would be too tall. Some dogs were high dollar dogs and some were mutts, but to their masters they were all champions. There were those described as walkers, black and tans, blue tick and lemon spotted. Hunters detested yard dogs that joined the races because they wouldn't bark to let them know when to expect the deer.

Each night at camp was spent playing cards, seeing who could tell the biggest yarn about the day's hunt and planning the next day's drives. All of the men who owned dogs took turns making drives with them. I don't know why they were called drives because they only drove with their dogs in the back of their truck to a selected spot. The dogs were usually in a homemade box or cage in the back of the truck. Everyone else was assigned a place to stand so that the entire area the dogs were to be running in was surrounded. Everyone would pile in truck to be left at his or her stand.

The idea was that if you didn't have a vehicle, you were less likely to leave your stand, which would leave a gap in the circle where a deer could escape. You were really griped at if you left your stand and the deer slipped through. This also allowed the dogs to get lost and the owners spent a lot of time looking for them.

More than a few times have hunters fallen asleep on their spot and messed things up too. There was something about getting up before daylight, eating a hearty breakfast and then sitting in a warm sunny spot on a frosty morning that made you sleepy. On more than one occasion I would be watching one direction and the deer would be seen crossing the road behind me.

Deer had their favorite crossing places you were to watch, but they could smell you and try another route around. Leaving your stand could pose a safety problem also, for the standers were placed a safe distance apart, so if you left your stand you would be within shooting distance of someone on either side of you.

Roadrunners who didn't get out of their vehicle to stand were detested. Their running the roads trying to get in front of a pack of dogs running a deer, turned the deer and kept it from crossing by someone who had stood all morning awaiting that great moment. There would be heated discussions if someone heard the dogs coming and had their gun raised with safety off, ready to shoot and all of a sudden a speeding vehicle came flying down the gravel road noisily causing the deer to turn in another direction.

There were those who described the excitement of the last moment before the deer crossed as a buckager. It was described as a nervous shake while in a cold sweat. If they got overexcited and their shot missed, there were all kinds of excuses. The gun jamming was a well-used one. I always figured they might have forgotten to take their safety off.

Sometimes shells were said to be old or it was too far to shoot. If the shot was successful, the distance between where they stood and the place the deer was shot was stepped off. Naturally the distance was greatly exaggerated. There were those such as my grandfather I would not have wanted shooting at me. He was well into his senior years and still killed deer from great distances.

Sometimes when all the dogs were tired or had been lost, we kids were recruited to make a deer drive through the woods with Dad. We whooped and hollered enough that any deer for miles around would run.

Deer antlers were the hunter's prized possessions from their kills. The total points were counted and the spread was measured. If it wasn't a really large set, they would be nailed to the front of the camp. When they killed a deer, it was draped over the front hood of the vehicle or on the tailgate of the truck for picture taking. Then it was rushed away to the store to tag it.

The store was the official place that kept the records of the deer harvest for the Game and Fish Commission. Some hunters would have the entire deer head mounted. I don't know if we couldn't afford it or if Mom wouldn't allow one to be hung over our fireplace.

At the end of the day anyone who had missed a deer had his or her shirttail cut off. My grandmother used these to piece a quilt top. If the hunter was lucky, he still had enough of a shirt left to wear. Some guys, however, took great joy in cutting out the entire back of a good shirt. One humiliated boy had to come back and request his shirttail because his Mom did not understand nor appreciate the tradition. She wanted to sew his shirttail back on. Years later he returned to hunt and he still had that same shirt.

There are so many funny stories I remember as a child at deer camp. One of my brothers was too young for school so he was kind of the camp mascot during the day. He was known to have a big imagination. Once while the men were in the camp eating, Eddie ran in excited and said there is a big buck out here on the pond. The great white hunters told him to shoot it, then. He grabbed his faithful B.B. gun and ran back out. Much to the men's surprise, they looked out and saw that he was cocking that gun as fast as his little hands could and was shooting repeatedly at a big buck not 20 feet from the front door. They never doubted the validity of his stories again.

Another day, my other brother Marvin was put out on his stand by Dad. A stray dog kept bothering him and he was afraid if a deer came close, the dog would spook it.

My dad came by to check on him and told him to scold the dog and get rid of it. Dad went on down the road to another stand but he could see Marvin.

Well, Scrooge, my pet name for Marvin, heard something in the brush and said to himself, this dog is going to get a swift kick this time. He put his gun down and crawled over to the brush with his hand outstretched and saying here puppy, puppy, puppy. My dad was watching and wondering what in the world he was doing playing on his stand and not paying attention.

About that time, it was apparent to Scrooge that it wasn't the dog he was hearing because a big buck deer jumped out at him and he didn't have his gun ready. I don't know which of the great white hunters this humiliated most. Dad couldn't shoot for fear of hitting his oldest man-child. They could have kept this story as a secret between themselves, but Dad had to share it with everyone for miles around and still does so today even though it happened probably 35 years ago.

One occurrence stands out in my mind. We were taught respect for the weapons and safety was stressed to the utmost. In my case though, the fun was just being included in the excitement. I was a pretty fair marksman, though I really don't think I could have killed a beautiful, brown-eyed deer. On this occasion, my poor Dad had all four of his offspring on a stand with him. All hunters make a mistake sometimes and shoot a doe when they think it's a buck. Dad took a pretty long shot and when we all piled in the old truck and sped down the road to the deer, we discovered it was a wounded doe with a shattered leg.

When it looked up at us kids with those big brown eyes, bleating and pleading for help, we all started to bawl like babies and begged Dad not to shoot again. We were sure we could nurse it back to health and keep it for a pet. Of course the end was inevitable. Now the question was how was he going to get four bawling kids, himself and an illegal deer in the front of the pickup.

We drove past the warden that day with four bawling kids, one irritated but patient hunter and an illegal deer behind the seat. Come to think of it, we had several close escapes.

Dad had taken all of us kids and a friend of mine back into the woods on an old logging road. He spaced us safely apart and went to his own stand (this time by himself). My friend and I got cold immediately and built a fire. We had such a smoky roaring fire, we couldn't have seen a deer if one would even have come close. Later in the morning we heard a shot, but knew better than to investigate because we were told to stay put.

We heard a vehicle and figured it was Dad coming to retrieve all of us. Two hunters drove up and asked if we knew a little, short, pudgy-faced boy who was down the road a little. I had to own up to the fact that, I thought, it was probably my youngest brother. They proclaimed that he needed some help. They too had heard the shots and went to investigate. They had stopped to ask Eddie if he had seen anything or knew who had shot. Having been warned of game wardens that might take him to jail, he said no.

The men told me his gun was lying on the ground, his hands were behind his back and he was trying to whistle as behind him two dogs were pulling on each end of the big doe he had killed. We hurried down to him and covered the deer with leaves. It seemed the deer had jumped off an embankment almost on top of him. I think he really shot out of self-defense. When Dad arrived, he put the deer in the back of an old car we had. When pulling out onto the highway, we again passed the game warden.

My other brother and I took a lot of teasing because our little brother had killed a deer before we did.

Chapter Twenty-One

Are We Fishing Again Or Is This A Real Vacation?

Our family never had the means to take family vacations when we were kids. I still haven't been to Disney World or a lot of other tourist attractions. Our leisure time, when we had some, was spent on camping trips with other families who had children. My being the oldest of the group of children had its disadvantages. I was the built-in babysitter and lifeguard. At one point in time our group of campers found a little group of rundown cabins in a secluded area right on a lake.

We spent several happy times at Wagner's landing. One of the cabins had a screened-in porch, which was labeled as the kid's sleeping territory. My friend and I slept on top of a table on air mattresses while the boys slept in lounge chairs. One morning we girls woke up stiff and sore because the boys had let the air out of our mattresses and we had slept on the hard table. An old iron bedstead our parents slept on usually fell flat on the floor at least once a night. There was no end to the excitement our group could muster up.

One day, my girlfriend and I ventured out on our own in a rowboat. We were close to the dam and when the gates opened we were swept further and further down the lake by the swift current. We paddled and paddled and couldn't make any progress. Dad finally came to our rescue just as darkness was falling. I think he just wanted to see if we would get scared or not.

It was here that my lifeguard abilities were tested to the utmost. Mom, being scared of water, was coaxed into putting on a ski belt so she could make her way out to the swimming dock where we kids were. She didn't fasten the belt properly and it floated off. She probably could have dog paddled her way to safety if she hadn't been so scared and got excited. At age fifteen I was very physically fit, but she gave me a hard time getting her in.

Fishing, fishing, fishing is what these trips meant to my Dad. In the early spring, he began to watch to see when the dogwoods began to bloom. When they were just right, it was supposed to be bass spawning time and away we would go.

A few times we have seen Dad get too anxious and he would end up fishing with snow flurries falling around the boat.

Year after year, we met new friends on these camping trips and continue to see them from time to time on the banks of the same old lakes and rivers. The competition between the fishermen was always hot and heavy. When the spawning season was just right, it was nothing for each boat to come back to camp with enough fish to completely cover a picnic table.

The cleaning would commence. Filet after filet would be added to the pile of fish that would be cooked at that day's camp fish fry. Each filet was rolled in salted cornmeal and dropped in the black cast iron Dutch oven of hot grease and fried to a crisp golden brown. The rest of the menu consisted of fried taters, pork n' beans, hushpuppies, coleslaw and onions. One of my uncles loved to drop canned biscuits into the hot grease. Everyone loved to eat these with honey for dessert.

The first camper was a homemade rig. Dad used the frame from an old trailer house and constructed a plywood camper on this frame. It looked like a big forest green cracker box. Inside he installed enough beds for all our family to sleep. The cooking was done outside. In one end, I had a small metal trundle bed. The two boys had army cots hanging from the wall by chains. In the other end the folks had a full-size bed with another army cot on the wall above it for my little sister.

There was one problem with this camper. It had a habit of tilting up on my end when everyone else was in his or her bed on the other end. It was hard for my parents to get out of bed when this happened and it was hard for me to stay in my bed when it happened. I guess we didn't have jacks then to put under the back end of the trailer.

After the homemade trailer was gone, there had steadily been a long history of camper after camper, motor home after motor home in my parents' lives. Now in their senior citizen days, after we left home, they have a camper large enough to live in.

We moved from our Tight Wad house when I was sixteen. That house still holds more good memories for me than where my parents still live in Sweet Home. The most memorable moment I remember about the new house was the night my brothers pulled back their bedspread and there was a rattlesnake lying across their pillows. Thankfully, Dad was at home. He didn't want to shoot up the new house and while he was thinking about what to do, the snake crawled off the bed and into the bedsprings. It was quite a task for him to get that angry snake out of those springs and do away with him. Evidently it had been carried into the house in one of our moving boxes that had been stacked on the carport.

In the 1960s our grandparents had their old house moved down the road for my aunt to live in and they had a new house built. Grandma and Grandpa's new house didn't have a sleeping porch so there was a shortage of beds when we stayed overnight. There was only one thing to do. We made Baptist pallets on the floor. My younger brother and I were on a pallet one night sound asleep. Scrooge was sleeping with Uncle Frank. Some time during the night I was rudely awakened because Scrooge was standing over me relieving himself in my face.

Naturally I started screaming and woke up everyone but Pa, because he couldn't hear it thunder without his hearing aid. When Uncle Frank asked Scrooge what he thought he was doing, he turned and aimed his stream right at Uncle Frank. Scrooge swears to this day that he was sleepwalking and in the old house you turned the opposite way to get to the bathroom than you did in the new one. He wasn't used to getting around in the new house in the dark, he said. That story had a few holes in it, don't you think? I hadn't thought about it until now, but he may have been getting even for my giving him that bloody nose in front of his friends.

Grandma didn't get to enjoy her first new house very long before she was bedridden and the cancer eventually became more than God wanted her to bear and he called her home. That left Grandpa and his bachelor son who was in his 50s and unmarried to keep house together. It was amazing how well they did on their own. Of course my aunts, Mom and a lot of other people in the community saw that they had plenty to eat and got fresh sheets on their beds each week.

Eventually that all ended when the bachelor took a wife. It was a hard transition for Grandpa. He was so used to being the boss and treating Uncle Frank like a child. He couldn't understand that now Uncle Frank couldn't jump up when Pa wanted him to go to the farm. They finally got a system going and things worked themselves out until Pa was in his late 90s and wasn't very cooperative anymore and needed the special attention he could get in the nursing home.

Chapter Twenty-Two

How You Live Your Life, Remains After You Are Gone

Even after their deaths, they still taught me something. In the eulogy at Grandpa's funeral, he was described as being content with his place in life. He wasn't interested in worldly possessions of silver and gold. As long as Pa had a place to sleep and food for his tummy he was satisfied.

On days that the weather was nice, Grandpa and Uncle Frank came to the farm. They would usually visit me and my man, as Grandpa called my husband. The length of their visit was based on whether Grandpa had forgotten his tobacco or not. When you saw him start patting around on his pockets and looking at his pocket watch, you knew he was going to announce it was time to go.

On one such visit they were watching my husband build a cattle guard. He had dug a deep and wide trench across the road. Naturally they wanted to be on the other side. Grandpa told Uncle Frank to jump it. Uncle Frank, who has a crippled leg, told Pa he couldn't jump that ditch. Grandpa said so seriously, "Wonder Woman could." We didn't realize until then that she was his new TV hero.

In earlier years he had worked hard to provide for his family. In his senior years his family did all they could to make him comfortable. He was content to sit in his recliner and enjoy his pipe while watching and waiting for the mailman. The weather was his main topic of conversation when you tried to initiate a conversation with him.

In his senior years, relating to people outside of the family was not easy for him. Even while Grandma was ill, he didn't like to eat while so many people were in the house. Finally Dad installed a drape between the living area and kitchen so Pa could eat in peace. As soon as he ate, he would sneak out the back door and find a more private place. During this time is when he preferred to visit the outhouse in the chicken yard. There were just too many people in the house for him to feel comfortable. Also, I feel that Grandpa was grieving because he realized his mate of all those years would soon be separated from him.

Not being able to hear was a handicap for him, I'm sure, but he never complained unless his hearing aid batteries went bad. Well, maybe I should take that statement back. When the nursing home became his home, one of the other residents stole the hearing aid. Pa said the culprit was a man with a wheel. Well, a wheel was what he usually called a bicycle. He finally got it across to me what he was talking about when he saw the little old thief pushing a wheelchair and he told me that's the man with a wheel.

We figured the old gent thought it was a radio. When we found it hidden in his wheelchair and in several pieces, there was nothing we could do but have Pa fitted for a new one. After that Pa hid it under his mattress at night. You might fool him one time, but even at his age, no one was going to fool him the second time.

I think the one thing that Pa missed the most while at the nursing home was his being able to smoke his pipe. We tried taking him to the designated smoking place, but that was too much trouble for him, so after that he opted to chew tobacco.

Probably 20 years after Grandma's death, I was visiting with the doctor who attended her during her long battle with cancer. What he said about her stuck with me. He said "That lady taught me a lot about humility and dying in a dignified way." Will I be able to face the Valley of the Shadow of Death the same way?

Even though Grandma's illness was a long and painful one, she tried to protect her family as long as she could. After losing one breast to that dreaded disease and knowing what the radiation treatment was like, she opted to keep the recurrence in her other breast a secret. She kept her strong faith in God and it showed throughout her suffering. The family and community that she had doctored and helped in their time of need now committed themselves to meeting her needs. Someone was there with her 24 hours a day. There was an endless supply of food brought each day. That was the community's way of saying that they cared. The Lord took her home when her suffering was too much for her to bear.

As I write, I am looking at a picture of her sitting in a straight-backed chair, scarf on her head with the ever-present apron on. At the same time I can see my own reflection in the mirror of her old dresser and marvel at how much my appearance grows closer and closer to hers with every passing year. If only my character and faith were as strong as that of Alice Edna "Reynolds" Roberts, the Wonder Woman of Sweet Home USA.

Chapter Twenty-Three

Gone But Not Forgotten, Yet!

Gone now is the landmark, a huge oak tree, known to everyone as "The Big Oak," which was Grandpa's deer stand. We fought to keep it from being cut when the highway was widened, but it died later anyway. The gristmill stone wheel is gone now, sold to be moved to Arizona. There are no hickory nuts to crack on it anyway, for the old tree is gone too.

I never go down the lane anymore, although it is still there, for the barn is also long gone and I drive to church instead of walking the trail through the woods. The drive to the cemetery isn't near as much fun now because the timber company has leased the land between the cemetery and us.

All of the country roads have locked gates on them and only hunting club members have a key. Going all the way around by the highway wouldn't have seemed fitt'n to Ben and Alice Roberts.

Their oldest child, Millie, has gone now to meet them at the pearly gates. Their three sons, Frank, George Calvin and Bennie Ray can all be considered as senior citizens now. At this time in their lives they are healthier in mind and body than some their age.

Shirley, the other daughter, had no choice but to leave the old house empty now. She has no recollection of the death of her beloved parents and her spouse of many years. Aunt Shirley now resides in a home that cares for those whose mind tricks them into living in the past instead of the present. Having taken care of someone all of her life, she just doesn't know how to accept that she only needs to care for herself now.

Although it is in another location, their house still stands, unoccupied now, to remind us of precious memories and how they linger.

Epilogue

A Challenge for Parents & Grandparents

These are but a few memories I have of growing up with these grandparents and I am proud to have this type of heritage. I have a fear of losing my memory; therefore, I choose to pass this knowledge and history along now. So many children do not have this type of relationship with their parents or grandparents. Parents and grandparents who may read this, I challenge you to give your children and grandchildren good memories that they will have throughout their lifetime. Even if you can teach them to respect their elders and to say yes ma'am and no ma'am, yes sir, no sir, please, thank you and you're welcome as my grandmother did, you will be giving them something they will never forget. Stop and think. If your child or grandchild becomes an author in the future, what will his or her manuscript say about you?

Acknowledgments

I must thank the entire Roberts clan for my raising. It took every one of them to mold and model my character to make it what it is now. Thanks to everyone else in the Sweet Home and Tight Wad area who also had an influence on my life. A very special thanks to my Dad and Mom and siblings, who helped refresh my memory on some points.

This book would never have come to print without the help of my editor, Allan G. Macpherson. You were extremely patient with me and provided me with the encouragement I needed. Thanks, Allan.

About The Author

Dennis, my husband of 30 years, and I still reside near Sweet Home, Arkansas. Our self-constructed home is located on property that was our family farm and deer camp during my childhood. As a child, I would look at this green field, shaded by a circle of huge, ancient, oak trees, daffodils wildly sprouting and blooming everywhere, the only reminder that a house once stood at that very location years ago. I would watch the cows as they lazed under the shade in the heat of the day, peacefully chewing their cud, and I'd dream of having a home there.

My childhood dream came true. Straight out of high school, I just happened to marry a man of many talents. He is very creative when it comes to building or inventing when he wants to. He wanted to build a home in my dream spot from the moment I first shared it with him. There are many memories, good and bad, that are connected with this dream coming true. In the blink of an eye, I can tell you true stories that will make you keel over in laughter, while the next moment you will be overwhelmed with tears when I relate how my only child died here tragically at an early age.

Now we are two people and their dog, Baby Doll, and recently acquired cat, Sassy, residing at Old Smokey Farm growing old together, watching the deer feast on the abundance of acorns.